Costing
and
Pricing
Public Sector
Services

Second Edition

Essential Skills for
the Public Sector

HB PUBLICATIONS

Jennifer
Lascelles

Costing and Pricing Public Sector Services

HB PUBLICATIONS
(Incorporated as Givegood Limited)

Published by:

HB Publications
London, England

First Published 1996 © HB Publications
Second Edition 2011 © HB Publications

British Library Cataloguing in Publication Data

ISBN 978-1- 899448-62-3

For further information see www.hbpublications.com
and www.fci-system.com

Contents

Chapter 1

INTRODUCTION

Costing and pricing public services is fundamental to achieving value for money, an objective now required by most public sector organisations seeking to work within increasingly constrained budgets. Many countries are currently facing budget deficits which are often curtailed by reducing public expenditure. This in turn has presented challenges in ensuring that important public services are still delivered, but at a reduced cost, and minimal compromise to quality

The identification of the true cost of a service is often the first stage in being able to establish whether or not the existing service delivery process is providing value for money. It enables costs to be compared with similar services elsewhere, and in some cases may provide justification for out-sourcing a service to a third party, and greater local accountability.

Some public services are very difficult to cost and compare due to their unique nature. However, despite this, knowing the cost of a service is the real starting point to efficient, effective and economic service delivery.

Certain public services may also need to establish a price. This may be as a result of being in a competitive market place, or it may be for re-charging purposes to internal customers. The approach to developing a price can be very similar to that adopted in the private sector, depending on the nature of the service and the objectives of the organisation.

This book has been developed to assist those working in the public sector to understand the concepts of costing and pricing, and how these concepts can be applied to their service areas. It is also relevant to those working in a voluntary sector or other non-commercial environment. It has been designed as a reference text and development tool which can be used by the reader as part of a self-development programme. It covers important concepts such as establishing the cost of a service; calculating unit costs; controlling costs; and pricing.

In order to make the contents of this book accessible to all, a simple format has been adopted with the emphasis on practical application as opposed to theory. At the conclusion of each chapter are exercises which help the reader to focus on the key issues covered. Suggested solutions have been given in the last section of the book, where appropriate.

This book is one of a series of "Essential Skills for the Public Sector" titles. The series aims to assist public sector managers become more efficient and effective in carrying out their important management responsibilities. We consider this book to be an important part of the tool kit for public sector management development.

Chapter 2

ESTABLISHING THE COST OF A SERVICE

Service Definition

In order to establish the cost of any type of service, there must first be a service definition. This definition sets out the content of the service in terms of its **description**, **quantity** and **quality**.

Service Description

The service description will outline the content and scope of the service. For example, a hospital will offer patient care for people of different ages, with a variety of ailments, along with a range of other supplementary services which may include créche facilities, shops, a café, and so on.

Service Quantity

Quantity covers all issues to do with size, opening hours, number of service units, number of users, etc. Service quantity in the case of a hospital will include the number of beds available for public and private use, the number of outpatients that can be seen, the visiting hours, etc.

Service Quality

Quality has to be defined and made known to staff and customers/users. The organisation has to ensure the quality standards stated are met at all times and this will have an

3

impact on resources. What is deemed to be an important quality issue will vary depending on the nature of the service. For example, in a hospital, waiting times may be a key quality standard to be adhered to.

The description, quantity and quality are all inter-related and have an impact on the resource requirements of the service.

The next stage is to identify exactly how the service definition can be fulfilled in terms of the necessary resources and their cost. These issues will be covered in the following section, "elements of service cost".

Elements of Service Cost

In order to deliver any service, there is a need to input a variety of resources. These will generally include the following elements:

❖ *Staffing*

❖ *Accommodation*

❖ *Goods and Services*

❖ *Fixtures, Fittings, and Equipment*

These resources will normally have a cost which is expressed in financial terms. Examples of resource inputs with related cost implications include:

Staff Related Costs

Salaries and wages (including on-costs)
Overtime
Temporary/Agency fees
Travel and subsistence

Property Related Costs

Rent and Rates
Services (cleaning, security, etc.)
Utilities (electricity, telephone and gas)

Goods and Services Costs

Materials
Printing and stationery
Postage
Training
Professional fees
Insurance
Support service costs (e.g. central cost of
personnel, legal, finance, etc.)
Interest charges (reflecting the cost of any
borrowing the service incurs)

Fixtures, Fittings and Equipment Costs

Office furniture
Computer hardware and software
Repairs and renewals

In order to calculate the actual cost of each element required to deliver the service, there is a need to "capture" costs.

Capturing Costs

The concept of capturing costs refers to the process which ensures all the correct costs, in their respective proportions, are included as part of the overall cost of a given service. This is essential if an accurate service cost is to be calculated. For example, if two distinct services are managed by the same individual, in order to properly reflect the manager's salary costs, it will be necessary to **apportion** the manager's salary between the two services.

Other costs that may need to be correctly captured include items such as the shared cost of accommodation, reception areas, insurance policies, central support service costs, and so on. Having captured all the costs relating to a particular service, or part of a service, a total or partial service cost can be established.

For most public sector organisations, staffing costs usually represent the most significant cost of service delivery. Where elements of staffing cost have to be apportioned, such as the manager described above, there is a need to identify an appropriate method of apportionment. In the case of staff, one method of apportionment is time (i.e. the amount of time spent undertaking elements of the service). Where time apportionment is deemed appropriate, then implementing a time recording system may be useful. The use of time recording is commonplace in the private sector and is becoming more common in the public sector.

The apportionment of costs, particularly overheads, is an important area of discussion. A number of techniques which may be applied to overhead apportionment are discussed in chapter 3.

In order to calculate the unit costs of a service, (which is discussed in chapter 4) there is a further need to split the total service cost between fixed and variable costs. Fixed and variable costs are discussed below.

Fixed Costs

A fixed cost is one that does not vary with service output in the short term. This means the cost of the resource will remain constant, regardless of the amount of service activity undertaken. This is illustrated in the following graph:

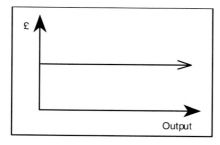

The vertical axis of the graph identifies the service cost in monetary terms, and the output or productivity of the service is represented by the horizontal axis. The output is identified as a number of units of service, which in turn is usually expressed in the most appropriate unit depending on the nature of the service, e.g. number of hours, number of interviews, number of applications, number of enquiries, number of people, etc.

The fixed cost line shows a consistent cost regardless of the number of units. A good example of a fixed cost is rent and rates as these costs are fixed for a certain level of accommodation. It does not matter how often the accommodation is used or the level of output produced, the rent and rates will remain the same. Salaries can be seen as another fixed cost. If an employee is paid a fixed salary for standard terms and conditions, then their salary will be the same regardless of the effort they put into their jobs, i.e. it will not be affected by their productivity or the number of hours spent working.

Fixed costs will normally only remain at the same level for a period of time, i.e. they will not vary with output in the short term. However, in the longer term the level of these costs may change, as the activity and scope of the service changes. For example, rent and rates are fixed costs, but if the service grows to a size where the current accommodation is insufficient, there may be a need to increase the amount of space used. Hence, the cost of rent and rates will increase to reflect the new accommodation requirements, and will result in a step up in fixed costs.

The following graph shows the step effect of changing fixed costs over time.

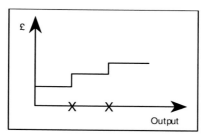

When X increases significantly there may need to be a step change in the level of costs, which once revised, will remain fixed for another range of output.

Variable Costs

Variable costs vary in relation to service output and activity. An example of a variable cost is the cost of temporary staff. Unlike a fixed cost, this cost is only incurred when temporary staff are engaged. In most cases, variable costs have a constant and direct relationship to output, however, in some instances the variable cost per unit of output can reduce over time with volume. For example, it is quite common to obtain volume discounts, or to negotiate improved rates for bulk purchasing.

A typical graph of variable costs is shown as follows:

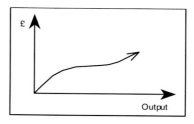

Variable costs increase with output.

9

Direct and Indirect Costs

Having discussed fixed and variable costs, it is important to distinguish the following terms:

Direct Costs

Any cost directly related to a specific product or service. These are usually variable in nature and include items such as materials. However, a fixed cost such as rent could also be a direct cost if expenditure on rent can be directly attributable to a specific product or service. For example, the renting of a particular machine used in the production process of a specific service or product

Indirect Costs

Any cost required to deliver the service that is not directly related to the service output. These are usually fixed and include items such as rent and salaries. However, they may also include variable costs such as the overtime of staff which cannot be directly attributable to the product/ service

The terms direct and indirect are sometimes used interchangeably with the terms fixed and variable. It is important to be clear of the difference between the two concepts and an illustration is given as follows:

Nursery School Places			
	Variable **£**	**Fixed** **£**	**Total** **£**
Direct Costs:			
Materials	10,000		10,000
Food	12,000		12,000
Sessional staff	6,000		6,000
Publicity	-	5,000	5,000
	28,000	5,000	33,000
Indirect Costs:			
Staff (including overtime)	6,000	120,000	126,000
Accommodation		15,000	15,000
Utilities		3,000	3,000
Telephone		1,500	1,500
Mini-bus		2,500	2,500
Other		1,000	1,000
	6,000	143,000	149,000
Total	34,000	148,000	182,000

The total direct costs are £33,000 and indirect costs are £149,000, whereas the total variable costs are £34,000 and the total fixed costs are £148,000.

Controllable and Uncontrollable Costs

Definitions of controllable and uncontrollable costs are given as follows:

Controllable Costs
Costs that can be stopped immediately at any time

Uncontrollable Costs
Costs which cannot be stopped in the short term and have to be incurred (even though all costs can be controlled in the longer term).

Variable costs are controllable, whereas fixed costs are generally uncontrollable in the short term and only controllable in the long term. However, there are some exceptions where fixed costs can be controlled in the short term. These include activities such as marketing, training and general printing.

Costs which fall in between the two definitions are called semi-controllable. Semi-controllable costs may not be completely stopped at any time, but can be dramatically changed. An example of a semi-controllable cost is the telephone bill. Call charges may be stopped immediately by the user ceasing to make further calls. However, the line or network rental (a fixed cost) may still have to be incurred for a specific period until the contract can be terminated. Similarly, if the handset is hired, the hire charge will continue subject to the terms of the hire agreement.

Identifying which costs are controllable and which are uncontrollable assists in cost control, monitoring and management. These issues are discussed in chapter 5.

Cost of Capital Investment

It is important to take the cost of capital into consideration when capturing all the relevant service costs. This cost relates to interest charged on loan finance and is sometimes referred to as a debt charge.

In order to establish a service, it is common to incur start-up costs which relate to the initial activities and expenses. Start-up costs include expenditure on capital items such as furniture, equipment, vehicles, and any initial research or exploratory work undertaken. This initial investment has to be financed, and it is the cost of this financing that has to be taken into account.

The cost of capital is a fixed cost because it does not vary with output, however, it may or may not be controllable. The extent to which interest payments can be controlled will depend on the nature of the loan agreements. Some loans have fixed term and fixed rate interest charges whereas others may have variable rates. It may also be possible to change interest charge and payment arrangements, and hence there can be an element of control in this area.

Sunk Costs

This term is used to describe **irrecoverable costs**. These include items such as the cost of aborted research and development, set up costs for a project that does not proceed, and so on. Sunk costs tend to be incurred when there is an element of risk attached to service development. If an organisation is in a position where it needs to directly recover all costs, including sunk costs, these will have to be absorbed within the costing process. They may have to be captured by a particular service or form part of a central cost which is then spread across a number of services. In the latter case, sunk costs fall into the general pot with other overhead costs. The apportionment of overheads is discussed in chapter 3.

Summary

❏ To establish the cost of any service, it is necessary to define the service in terms of content, quantity and quality

❏ To calculate the cost of a service, all the costs of the resources required to deliver the service need to be "captured"

❏ Fixed costs do not vary with service output, whereas variable costs do vary directly with service output

❏ Direct costs can be directly attributed to a specific service or product and are usually variable in nature

❏ Controllable costs can be stopped at any time, unlike uncontrollable costs. All costs can eventually be controlled in the long term

❏ There is a cost attached to the use of capital which should be taken into account when calculating a service cost

Exercise 1

Types of Cost

Identify the relevant cost categories for each area of expenditure.

(Tick the appropriate columns)

Area of Expenditure	Fixed Cost	Variable Cost	Direct Cost	Indirect Cost	Controllable Cost	Uncontrollable Cost (in the short term)
Salaries (full time staff)	☐	☐	☐	☐	☐	☐
Employee on costs*	☐	☐	☐	☐	☐	☐
Wages (full time staff)	☐	☐	☐	☐	☐	☐
Overtime	☐	☐	☐	☐	☐	☐
Agency fees (temp. staff)	☐	☐	☐	☐	☐	☐
Travel to clients	☐	☐	☐	☐	☐	☐
Leased cars	☐	☐	☐	☐	☐	☐
Rent	☐	☐	☐	☐	☐	☐
Repairs	☐	☐	☐	☐	☐	☐
Cleaning office premises	☐	☐	☐	☐	☐	☐
Security	☐	☐	☐	☐	☐	☐
Marketing	☐	☐	☐	☐	☐	☐
Printing	☐	☐	☐	☐	☐	☐
Stationery	☐	☐	☐	☐	☐	☐
Postage to clients	☐	☐	☐	☐	☐	☐
Equipment rental	☐	☐	☐	☐	☐	☐
Telephone calls	☐	☐	☐	☐	☐	☐
Sundries	☐	☐	☐	☐	☐	☐
Support service recharge	☐	☐	☐	☐	☐	☐
Debt charges	☐	☐	☐	☐	☐	☐

Some answers will vary depending on the type of activity
*Includes National Insurance and pension costs

Suggested solutions can be found on page 124

Exercise 2

Capturing Your Own Costs

List the key elements of costs incurred in order to deliver your service. Where possible, obtain accurate information, or otherwise make estimates of the costs and calculate a final cost of service.

Area of Cost	Amount (£)
Salaries	£ ....
Rent	£ ....
....	£ ....
....	£ ....
....	£ ....
....	£ ....
....	£ ....
....	£ ....
....	£ ....
....	£ ....
....	£ ....
....	£ ....
Total Service Cost	£

Chapter 3

OVERHEAD COSTS

Types of Overhead Cost

The term "overheads" refers to a whole range of costs and is often used in different ways within different organisations. The Oxford dictionary definition of overheads is:

> "expenses arising from general running costs, as distinct from particular business transactions"

Overheads are generally fixed in nature and include a combination of controllable and uncontrollable costs, and may be broken down into a number of categories which are discussed as follows:

Accommodation
This includes all costs relating to the provision of the accommodation e.g. rent, rates, heat, light, security, cleaning, repairs and maintenance as well as other services relating to premises.

Telephones
There will be a line rental, and the equipment may be purchased or hired. Many organisations would consider all the costs relating to telephones, including the calls, to be an

overhead. This is because these costs cannot generally be directly attributable to specific services or products. However, some organisations use sophisticated systems that are able to record and allocate all calls to specific service areas accordingly.

Support Services

This heading covers all the other services that are required to successfully run an organisation. These include areas such as finance, personnel, legal, administration, purchasing, printing and so on. These services may be provided centrally by in-house departments and act as cost centres in their own right. As such, they are then treated as overheads by direct service departments.

Marketing

Like administration, there is often an organisational approach to marketing. Marketing is often provided centrally to ensure a consistent corporate strategy and identity. Certain aspects of marketing may be devolved on a service or product basis and may be directly attributable to the cost of the service or product.

Borrowing

Most organisations borrow money in order to invest in assets such as buildings, furniture and equipment. The cost of borrowing, usually referred to as interest or debt charges, has to be recovered. These costs usually form part of the overheads that have to be borne by each service/product area.

Management

Most organisations normally have a structure which incorporates a management tier or tiers. Management play a key role in leading, managing and monitoring the organisation's performance. The cost of management is usually viewed as an overhead.

Methods of Apportionment and Allocation

The overhead categories previously described, illustrate the range of overheads that need to be absorbed into the cost of the service or product. In order to successfully capture these costs, the overheads have to be allocated to each service area using a sensible method of apportionment.

Some of the main methods of apportionment are discussed on the following pages:

Method of Apportionment	Method of Allocation	Advantages	Disadvantages
Flat rate	Overheads allocated equally between each service or product area. Calculation takes total overheads divided by the number of service areas.	❖ Quick ❖ Easy ❖ Ensures overheads are fully absorbed into the cost of direct services	❖ Unfair, as allocation is not based on overhead usage ❖ Can heavily distort the cost of services, making some services seem very expensive and un-competitive, and others undervalued ❖ Provides no incentive to control overhead costs because they are fully charged out to services on an arbitrary basis

Method of Apportionment	Method of Allocation	Advantages	Disadvantages
Square footage	Overheads allocated in proportion to the amount of floor space occupied by the service.	❖ Quick ❖ Easy ❖ Very appropriate for accommodation costs	❖ Not appropriate for many types of overheads, and yields the same disadvantages as the flat rate method ❖ Even in the case of accommodation costs, it may unfairly penalise services occupying central accommodation which is not being efficiently utilised, e.g. having to contribute to empty office space.
Employee numbers	Overheads allocated in proportion to the number of staff engaged in each service area.	❖ Quick ❖ Easy ❖ Appropriate for staff related overheads such as personnel costs	❖ Same disadvantages as for the flat rate method ❖ No account usually taken of the different grades of staff engaged in the various services
Employment costs	Overheads allocated in proportion to the cost of employees engaged in each service area.	❖ Quick ❖ Easy ❖ Appropriate for staff related overheads such as personnel costs	❖ Same disadvantages as for the flat rate method ❖ No account taken of the number of staff engaged in each service area

21

Method of Apportionment	Method of Allocation	Advantages	Disadvantages
Budget size	Overheads allocated in proportion to the direct expenditure budget of each service area.	❖ Easy ❖ Quick ❖ The largest budget holder absorbs the largest proportion of the overheads. This may be considered to be an equitable approach	❖ Unfair, as allocation is not based on overheads used ❖ Can heavily distort the cost of services, making some services seem very expensive and un-competitive, and others undervalued ❖ Provides no pressure to control overhead costs because they are fully charged out to services on an arbitrary basis
Capital asset values	Overheads allocated in proportion to the assets used in the delivery of the service.	❖ Suitable for overheads relating to property and equipment such as maintenance, and depreciation ❖ Return on Capital is often used as a performance measure and this method directly reflects this measure	❖ May be difficult to estimate asset values, particularly if a service has inherited old assets ❖ Not suitable for overheads that have no relationship to the assets used ❖ If used as a general method, the highest overhead costs will be charged to the most capital intensive service, which has no bearing on the usage of overheads, or the contribution being made by the service to the organisation

Method of Apportionment	Method of Allocation	Advantages	Disadvantages
Output	Overheads allocated in proportion to the units of service output. In order to use this method, the unit of output would have to be common across all services, for example, numbers of productive hours.	❖ Links overheads to productivity levels. Reductions in productivity levels should therefore lead to reduced overheads (although there is normally a time lag) ❖ Ensures that output is monitored and records kept ❖ Forms a basis for developing pricing schedules for certain types of service	❖ Requires good record keeping in order to identify output levels ❖ If output levels are below the rates that need to be delivered, there may be an under-recovery of overheads by the year end ❖ Possibly no relationship between overheads allocated to the service unit cost and overheads utilised by the service
Actual usage	Overhead calculation based on how much of the overhead is used in the service. This method of allocation tends to require an internal charging system.	❖ Overhead costs directly related to the amount of overheads used by the service ❖ Ensures that overheads are scrutinised at service level, and are therefore usually minimised and more strictly controlled ❖ Requires certain overheads, such as support services, to justify the service they provide	❖ Requires a mix of different apportionment methods depending on the type of overhead, hence, a complex system of charging required, with some calculations being very complicated ❖ Some services may not be economically viable if they have to support the full cost of overheads utilised by the service

Actual usage is the fairest and most appropriate method to apportion overheads to service areas or cost centres. In addition, this allows service providers the most control over their costs. In order to facilitate this approach, many organisations establish internal charging mechanisms which are supported by other systems such as **service level agreements, trading accounts, time recording**, and so on. The following table identifies different overhead costs and the most appropriate method of allocation in each case.

Types of Overhead	Method of Allocation
Accommodation costs	Square footage - floor area of the service should be managed, and a square footage rate applied
Telephone costs	The rental costs are based on the actual number of lines and handsets used by the service. Calls should be monitored and charged according to the exact cost of each call made by the service
Marketing costs	If undertaken by a central department, should be charged on a job by job basis, e.g. each service should pay for the total cost of producing a leaflet. Other marketing activities could be charged on an hourly rate, or retainer basis
Support service costs	As for marketing, charges should be made on a job basis or on an hourly rate as used by the service area
Borrowing costs	Costs should be calculated for each service on the exact level of borrowing utilised. Borrowing could relate to specific capital assets purchased for use by the service
Management costs	Should be charged according to the amount of time spent by management on the service concerned

In some organisations where overheads are being allocated on a usage basis, problems have occurred when support services attempt to charge out their "true" costs to direct service areas. This arises because the support costs are affected by input costs from other support services, and a circular effect is produced.

Example

A personnel department requires finance services that in turn need personnel services. Neither can establish their full costs without the input cost of the other department.

Some strategies to solve the problem for support services are suggested as follows:

a) Combine all internal support services, such as legal, finance, personnel, etc. as one umbrella department. The combined department then recovers it's cost by charging to the direct service departments based on usage, ensuring that charge out rates are set at levels that can recover all their costs

b) Each support service to establish appropriate **fixed** charges for other support service divisions, to enable the calculation of their cost. These charges may not exactly equate to the service usage of the division. Charges to direct service departments should then be recovered on a usage basis, set at a level that recovers the fixed input costs of other support services

c)   Each support service department to provide an **estimated** cost to the other support services, on the basis of **expected** usage for the purpose of calculating unit costs.   As in (b), each support service should then recover their cost on a usage basis to direct service departments.   They should also maintain an account of the actual usage of service by the other support service divisions, and calculate a balancing charge at the year end to represent the over or under recovery of costs

Summary

❑   Overheads are usually fixed in nature and consist of controllable and uncontrollable costs

❑   There are many methods of apportionment such as square footage used, and employee numbers. All have advantages and dis-advantages

❑   Ideally overheads should be allocated to service areas based on usage

❑   Allocation methods will vary depending on the nature of the overhead, for example accommodation costs should be allocated to services based on the amount of space they occupy occupied

❑   All organisations have to incur overhead costs, which should be absorbed into the unit cost calculation

Exercise 3

Allocating Costs

A personnel service has identified its total costs as £800,000 for a year. This service represents an overhead to other departments and needs to establish a simple way to allocate its costs. There are eight direct service departments and in the past personnel have simply divided their costs equally across all eight and charged them £100,000 each. However, at least two of the service departments are about to test the market to establish if they receive value for money, and whether or not these services should be subjected to some form of competition. As a result, these departments, and others, have complained about the level of charges they have incurred and consider the method of apportionment being used is unfair.

You have the following information about each of the service departments:

Service Department	Employee Numbers	Employment Costs £'000	Budget Size £'000
1	200	4,000	8,000
2	250	3,500	8,000
3	390	3,900	6,500
4	160	3,600	4,000
5	125	1,500	3,000
6	400	6,000	7,000
7	325	5,200	5,800
8	150	1,800	2,500
Total	2,000	29,500	44,800

You consider that it is currently impossible to estimate the usage of the personnel service by department, but it may be fairer to apportion the costs in line with employee numbers, employee costs, or budget size.

In order to help with the decision making, you have been asked to select which method of apportionment you consider to be most appropriate. Use the following worksheet to calculate the new personnel cost allocation for each method.

Service Department	Employee Numbers	Personnel Cost £'000	Employment Costs £'000	Personnel Cost £'000	Budget Size £'000	Personnel Cost £'000
1	200		4,000		8,000	
2	250		3,500		8,000	
3	390		3,900		6,500	
4	160		3,600		4,000	
5	125		1,500		3,000	
6	400		6,000		7,000	
7	325		5,200		5,800	
8	150		1,800		2,500	
Total	2,000		29,500		44,800	

Suggested solutions can be found on page 125

Exercise 4

Your Overhead Costs

Consider the following questions:

a)   **Are overheads allocated to your service on a usage basis, or on an arbitrary method of apportionment?**

b)   **List the current overheads charged to your service. Then identify which, from your perspective, are fair, unfair, or should not be charged to your service area at all.**

Overhead	Fair	Unfair	Should not be charged
1.			
2.			
3.			
4.			
5.			
6.			
7.			
8.			
9.			
10.			

c)   In respect of any overheads identified as "unfair" or "should not be charged", consider what action could be taken to correct the imbalance.

OVERHEAD	ACTION
....	....
....	....
....	....
....	....
....	....
....	....
....	....
....	....
....	....
....	....
....	....
....	....
....	....

Chapter 4

CALCULATING UNIT COSTS

Unit of Service

A unit cost is the cost of *one unit of service*. There are many methods of calculating unit costs and these are usually determined by the unit of service. The unit of service selected depends on the following criteria:

> **The type of service**
> **The reason for calculating unit cost**
> **The ease of calculation**

Type of service

In the case of professional services, the most common unit of service is time. Many services are sold by the hour, and it is usual for charges to be quoted as hourly rates. This includes most professional activities such as legal, accountancy, and medical services. Where services can be defined into specific activities, they are sometimes sold as a specific unit. For example, a solicitor may quote a fixed price for conveyance, and an accountant may give a fixed price for the completion of a tax return. In order to establish the fee to be charged for fixed price activities, the cost per hour and the average time taken to complete the activity requires calculation. Another common way of pricing services is a *per person* approach. This approach is typically used by the leisure, hotel, and transport industries.

Most public sector activities are **service orientated** as opposed to **product based**. Whereas the unit of service is usually easily identified in a product based activity, it is not always as clear for a service.

The following table shows common units of service for different types of activity.

Type of Service	Common Unit of Service	Other Appropriate Units of Service
Professional services (e.g. legal, personnel, finance, architects, etc.)	per hour	per activity of the professional, e.g. per appointment/ session, per case, per project
Residential services (e.g. children's homes, homes for the elderly, nursing homes)	per person per week	per room, per year
Catering services (e.g. canteens, buffets, meals on wheels, etc.)	per item	per head, per meal
Leisure services (e.g. theatres, leisure centres, parks)	per person	per session, per visit, per year
Protective services (e.g. fire service, police service, environmental service)	per activity, per hour	per job, per callout, per visit

Type of Service	Common Unit of Service	Other Appropriate Units of Service
Educational services (e.g. schools, colleges)	per student	per session, per hour, per year
Housing services (e.g. housing management, housing repairs)	per dwelling	per person, per job, per hour
Health services (e.g. hospitals, clinics, doctors surgeries)	per person	per activity, per session, per hour
Revenue services (e.g. cash collection, debt collection)	per transaction	per activity, per person
Corporate and support services	per hour	per activity, per person

Reason for calculating unit cost

There are a number of reasons for calculating unit costs. These include the following:

❖ *To establish whether or not the service appears to be good value for money*

❖ *To develop a basis for the establishment of prices for external markets*

❖ *To undertake cost comparisons with alternative providers*

❖ *To undertake cost comparisons with other services*

❖ *To set targets for productivity, e.g. number of hours, clients, meals, etc.*

❖ *To identify options for cost reduction*

❖ *To create an internal market for services*

The unit of service selected will vary with the reason for the cost calculation. If the reason is to compare the prices of alternative providers, the unit of service chosen must be commonly used in the market place, such that the competitive position can be established on a like for like basis. If the unit cost is to be used for comparison across services, then a common unit needs to be taken that is appropriate to the different types of service, such as an hourly rate. The unit of service selected will often be that which appears most favourable when the unit cost calculation is made. A service may have a high cost per hour, but a relatively low cost per person (or other unit of activity depending on the numbers). For example, a 6 hour training day may cost £600, i.e. £100 per hour, whilst the cost for 12 participants would be £50 each for the day. The latter unit cost would appear to be better value for money even though the total service cost is the same.

Ease of calculation

Some units of service are easier to calculate than others. For example, hourly rates may prove impossible to calculate accurately if there are no time recording systems in existence to identify time usage. The process of establishing a time recording system may prove expensive and time consuming, therefore, this method may be impractical. The service may decide to use an alternative method, such as *cost per client* if the information is more readily and easily obtainable.

Methods of Unit Costing

There are many methods for calculating unit costs, some of which are straightforward and others more complex. All the methods described below will follow a *"full absorption cost"* principle. This means that all costs relating to the service, including all overhead costs, have to be absorbed into the calculation of the unit cost. The methods of costing to be described are as follows:

> **Flat rate costing**
> **Hourly rate costing**
> **Standard costing**
> **Job costing**
> **Process costing**

Flat rate costing

This is the simplest method of costing and is commonly adopted as a starting point to provide some idea of unit costs. This method takes the total cost of the service over a particular time frame and divides it by the total number of units of service delivered in that time frame. This method can be used for a whole service or a single activity. Examples are given as follows:

Flat rate cost of a regional health service per annum

Total cost	£40,000,000
Total population	2,000,000
Total users of the service	500,000

Cost per person in the area	£20 per annum (40,000,000÷2,000,000)
Cost per user	£80 each (40,000,000÷500,000)

Flat rate cost of an English class (2 hours)

Total cost	£300
Number of pupils	30
Cost per pupil	£10 (£300÷30)
Cost per pupil per hour	£5

This example shows, the calculation is easy once the total cost has been established and the unit of service determined. There are a number of advantages and dis-advantages to this approach which are summarised as follows:

Advantages	Dis-advantages
❑ Useful for general comparisons	❑ Not specific
❑ Broad brush calculation of value for money	❑ Can be misleading
❑ Quick and easy to calculate	❑ Poor value for money activities may be hidden when they are aggregated as part of a total service
❑ Can be used as an overall benchmark	

Hourly rate costing

Within this general heading are a number of ways to calculate a cost per hour. This method of costing is very important because it underpins many other costing methods which depend on hourly rate costs. Hourly rates are a very common unit cost for services where a tangible or defined output is not easily identifiable. The types of hourly rate calculations described include:

Flat Rate per Hour
Differential Rates per Hour

Flat Rate per Hour

Flat rate per hour is based on the same principles as the flat rate described earlier. It is calculated by taking the total cost of the service and dividing it by the total hours available; this gives an average rate per hour.

For example, a personnel division may cost £250,000 to deliver a range of services. Assuming that there are 4 professional staff, a manager, and an administrator, the total hours available could be considered to be: 6 (number of staff) x 35 (number of hours in the working week) x 52 (number of weeks in the year); a total of 10,920 hours. If the full costs are reflected in terms of available hours then the flat rate per hour is:

$$\frac{£250,000}{10,920} \quad = \quad £22.89 \text{ per hour}$$

Although this is a valid calculation, by aggregating all staff hours, no account has been taken of the individual positions and functions of those staff. Some staff will be directly engaged in the delivery of services whereas others may play a supporting role, and hence would not be employed if there were no staff engaged in direct service delivery. Also by totalling all the hours available in a year, there is no account taken of the unproductive hours that cannot be employed in service delivery. Unproductive hours include time spent on:

- *holidays*
- *sick leave*
- *meetings*
- *certain types of administration*

When calculating a flat hourly rate, it is common practice to only use the number of hours that relate to the *productive* time of those staff engaged in direct service delivery.

In the example given, it is likely that the professional staff and the manager will be involved in direct service delivery, however, the proportion of time might vary for each staff member. It can be assumed that the administrator provides a supporting role to the other staff and therefore their hours are not included in calculating the total.

Assume that the professional staff have 30 days annual leave and public holidays, 10 days sick leave, and at least 20% of their remaining time is spent in meetings and on administration. The manager has the same annual and sick leave, but spends 50% of the remaining time on meetings, administration and management duties. The total hours available for service delivery (productive time) will be calculated as follows:

Professional Staff

No. of working days in the year	260	(52 weeks x 5 days)
Less days annual and sick leave	-40	
Net working days	220	

Assuming a 7 hour day, the number of hours available for each professional member of staff to undertake productive activities is:

$$220 \ \times \ 7 \ \times \ 80\% \ = \ 1{,}232$$

Manager

Net working days will be the same as that of the professional staff, however the percentage available for direct service delivery will only be 50% as opposed to 80%, hence the managers available hours are:

$$220 \ \times \ 7 \ \times \ 50\% \ = \ 770$$

The total hours of productive time for direct service delivery are then used as the basis for the calculation as follows:

$$\frac{\text{Cost of service}}{\text{Total hours of productive time}}$$

$$\frac{£250,000}{5698*}$$

$$=$$

£43.88

* this is calculated by multiplying the professionals' productive hours by 4, and adding the managers' time, i.e. (4 x 1232) + 770

This calculation shows a very different cost per hour compared to the initial calculation, and identifies how the assumptions about available productive hours can affect the unit cost. This is the case for all services where hours are to be the main unit of service. The cost per hour is often used in other unit costing calculations as will be shown later in this chapter.

Differential Rates per Hour

Depending on the nature of the service and how unit costs are to be used, a flat rate per hour is not always a suitable method of unit costing. In the above example, the manager's cost per hour is the same as the professionals. This is often considered an inaccurate reflection of true costs because the manager is normally paid a higher salary and therefore costs the organisation more. The cost of managers, and their relative productivity and contribution to the organisation can be disguised by using a flat rate approach. Hence, one way of differentiating hourly rates is to take into account the grades of individual staff members by virtue of their differing salaries.

Within the private sector, hourly rates tend to be related to grades, even though there may be salary differentials within grades. In such cases, an average salary for the grade is taken to estimate cost per hour, and usually a cost plus approach to pricing is taken towards establishing the hourly rates to be charged to customers. Pricing techniques are covered in chapter 6. The process of differentiating the cost per hour, based on salary, can be undertaken in several ways. Two approaches are described in the following examples:

Cost of Personnel Division

	£	
Salaries	150,000	Includes 4 professional staff on average annual salaries of £25,000, a manager on £35,000 and £15,000 for the administrator
Other costs	100,000	Includes accommodation, telephone, utilities, materials, and so on
Total	**£ 250,000**	

In the previous example, the number of productive hours was identified as that of the professionals and manager added together. The administrator will for the purpose of this costing calculation, be treated as an "other cost". This is because the administrator's salary has to be absorbed by the productive time as with other overheads.

Method 1 – Overhead recovery rate

The first method of calculating differential unit costs is to separate the salaries of the productive staff from all other costs utilised in service delivery. In this example:

£100,000 + £15,000   =   £115,000
(Other costs plus the cost of the administrator)

When this split is made, these costs can be spread equally over all the productive labour hours. The rationale for this approach is to show that for every productive hour delivered, there is an element of overhead and support cost relating to that hour. This calculation would be:

Cost of overheads and support
Total hours of productive time

£115,000
5698
=
£20.18

This figure is sometimes referred to as an "overhead recovery rate" and is added to the cost per hour of each grade of staff.

Method 2- Overhead recovery percentage

This method adds an overhead "recovery percentage" to the productive hours. This is calculated by identifying what percentage of the productive employee costs are overhead and support costs. The same percentage is then added to the cost of each productive hour of each grade of staff. In this example, the overhead recovery percentage would be:

Cost of overheads and support
Cost of productive time

£115,000
*£135,000
=
85.2%

* Salary cost of manager and professionals

The cost per hour for each staff member will be differentiated by virtue of using the salary as the basis for the calculation and adding the overhead recovery rate or percentage. The salary cost per hour of staff responsible for delivering direct services is as follows:

Grade	Salary Cost *	Productive Hours	Salary Cost Per Hour
Manager	£35,000	770	£45.45
Professional	£25,000	1232	£20.29

*   Salary costs should include on-costs and any other staff related costs such as leased cars

The full cost per hour will now include the salary cost and the overhead recovery rate or percentage. The following table sets out the different costs per hour that result from the two approaches.

Grade	Base Salary Cost Per Hour	Overhead Recovery Rate	Cost per Hour (A)	Overhead Recovery %	Cost Per Hour (B)
Manager	**£45.45**	£20.18	£65.63	85.2%	£84.19
Professional	**£20.29**	£20.18	£40.47	85.2%	£37.58

It can be seen from the above, the two methods of overhead allocation produce a difference in the hourly rates of the manager and professionals, as compared to the single flat rate of £43.88. However, cost per hour B, gives a far greater differential between the manager and professional than cost per hour A. This demonstrates how changing the method of calculation can produce very different results. All the above approaches are valid, but the choice of approach will depend on the range of factors mentioned earlier in the chapter.

Once the cost per hour has been calculated, the figure can be used to ensure the number of productive hours produces revenues equal the total service costs.

Using Cost per Hour (B)

| Manager
(770 x £84.19) | + | 4 Professionals
(1232 x £37.58) | = | £250,021* |

* The slight difference of £21 is due to rounding differences throughout the calculation process

A common variation to this calculation is to add the unproductive portion of the manager and professionals' salary to the support costs, which is 50% of the manager's salary and 20% of the professionals' salary. The salary cost per hour for the manager and professionals is then based on 50% of the managers' salary and 80% of the professionals' salary. This again produces different results as follows:

Grade	Base Salary Cost Per Hour	Overhead Recovery Rate	Cost Per Hour (C)	Overhead Recovery %	Cost Per Hour (D)
Manager	£22.73 (17,500÷770)	£26.76 (*152,500÷5698)	£49.49	156.4% (152,500÷97,500**) x 100	£58.28
Professional	£16.23 (20,000÷1232)	£26.76 (*152,500÷5698)	£42.99	156.4% (152,500÷97,500**) x 100	£41.61

* £115,000 + 4 x 20% x £25,000 + 50% x £35,000 = £152,500
**£20,000 x 4 + £17,500 = £97,500

It is possible to adopt other approaches to calculating cost per hour, including:

- Differentiating the proportion of overheads attributed to each grade of staff on the basis that higher paid staff use more of the other resources, e.g. have a larger

office, have more access to administrative support, and
so on.

- Differentiation of the proportion of overheads attributed
to each grade of staff on the basis of the type of service
they are primarily engaged in. Some services utilise
more resources than others, e.g. more equipment, more
accommodation, and so on.

Standard costing

It is only possible to calculate the **actual** unit cost of a service
historically, when all the costs incurred in service delivery and
the units of output can be properly identified. The actual unit
costs may be higher or lower than the planned unit costs which
are based on budgeted service costs and planned output levels.
For example, the cost per hour calculations shown previously
were based on an estimated service cost, and estimated average
hours of productivity. In order to calculate the actual cost per
hour, time sheets may have to be kept to establish the actual
hours of productive time delivered by staff, and the financial
and management accounts maintained to record the true costs
incurred.

A standard cost is one form of planned unit cost, and is
relevant for standard activities which can be repeated in the
same way over and over again. Standard costs are often used
as part of the cost control process as they are compared with
actual costs. As with budgetary control, variances from the
standard costs can then be monitored and any problems acted
upon.

As explained earlier, there are many ways to calculate unit costs. Due to the nature of many public sector services, unit costs are often expressed in terms of time; public services are dependent on people for their delivery, unlike a manufacturing organisation where elements such as raw materials, machine time, packaging, distribution and so on are very important to the cost of the product.

Example
There are two council estates both with 5,000 dwellings, and both with repairs budgets of £1,000,000. The standard cost of repairs per dwelling is, therefore, £200 for both estates. However, historic data shows that council estate A has an average of 10,000 repairs undertaken each year, whereas council estate B has 8,000 repairs. This means the standard cost of a repair on estate A is £100 and the standard cost of a repair on estate B is £125. If there are valid reasons for the differences, the repairs manager should be monitoring the actual cost per repair against the standard average cost relevant for each estate, whilst ensuring that the standard cost of repairs per dwelling was the same for both estates, i.e. £200.

The above case provides a general approach to standard costs. To continue the theme of housing repairs, it is possible to create standard costs for a range of repairs such that a schedule of costs is developed, which can be used for monitoring and control. These schedules are sometimes used as a basis for price setting and the preparation of a "schedule of rates", and an example is shown in the following table:

Nature of Repair	Standard Time (hrs)	Standard Rate per Hour (£)	Labour Cost (£)	Standard Materials Cost (£)	Sub-total (£)	Overhead Recovery @ 100%	Total Cost (£)
Hanging a door	4	12	48	70	118	118	236
Window replacement	2	10	20	10	30	30	60
Changing a lock	1	10	10	5	15	15	30
Sealing a burst pipe	2	12	24	12	36	36	72

From the table, depending on the type of repair, an average time has been established to complete the work, and an average hourly rate has been calculated for the grade of staff assigned to each task. The average cost of materials for each activity has been identified and then a sufficient uplift is made to cover all the overheads incurred by the service. The total cost column is then monitored for each assignment.

Each repair is likely to incur different actual costs to that stated on the standard cost profile. Differences will occur if the repair takes longer, or if the materials used are more or less expensive. The manager is able to monitor performance and identify trends away from the standard cost such that necessary action to correct matters is taken. This approach can be used as an incentive for staff to complete their work within the standard time.

Job costing

This method of costing tends to be used by trades such as builders, engineers, architects, and so on. It is suitable for any service that works primarily on a project or contract basis.

Each job is specified and an agreement reached as to the nature of the work. Each job is then individually costed based upon the specification. In order to formulate the costs on as accurate a basis as possible, research should be undertaken with respect to all the inputs required for the job, including overheads. A cost plus approach could then be taken to establishing the price of the job. (See Pricing, Chapter 6)

When the price of a job has been quoted, it is usually fixed. Therefore, the actual cost of the job has to be closely monitored to ensure that it does not exceed the quoted price, as this would result in a loss or deficit. Job costing in some organisations can be very time consuming and can become an area of expertise in itself.

Process Costing

This technique is used where the unit of service is the result of a process. This occurs where the output from one stage of the process is the input to another stage. In order to adopt this technique, the service has to be broken down into a number of stages. Each stage is then individually costed to calculate the final unit of service cost. The following diagram illustrates the process costing approach.

Process Cost for Delivering a Foster Care Placement

Stage	Process	Input Cost		Output Cost
Stage 1	Assessment of child's needs	• Assessors time for assessing and report preparation; 14 hours @ £50		£700
Stage 2	Registration of foster carer	• Input cost from Stage 1 • Recruitment cost per person • Assessment Time; 7 hours @ £50 • Training cost per person • Panel interview time per person	700 400 350 250 200	1,900
Stage 3	Matching foster carer to child	• Input cost from stage 2 • Case review time; 4 hours @ £50 • Foster carer selection time; 10 hours @ £50	1,900 200 500	2,600
Stage 4	Co-ordinating the placement	• Input cost from stage 3 • Transport costs • Set up costs • Social worker time; 4 hours @ £50	2,600 100 500 200	3,400
Stage 5	Monitoring the placement for a year	• Input cost from stage 4 • Social worker time (including visits, reports, etc.); 48 hours @ £50 • Transport costs • Foster carer support meetings • Foster carer fees; £100 per week • Child allowances; £25 per week • Re-assessment (same as stage 1 in process)	3,400 2,400 200 400 5,200 1,300 700	13,600
	Cost per placement per annum (total of all stages of the process)			<u>13,600</u>

Marginal Costing

The marginal cost of a unit of service is the cost of "*one more*" unit of service. This is a different approach to considering the full unit cost (i.e. the full absorption approach) which has been covered in previous sections. The marginal cost looks at the incremental cost of the next unit of service.

In order to calculate the marginal cost, the costs have to be split into their fixed and variable components. The previous chapter distinguished fixed costs as those costs that do not vary with output, whereas variable costs do vary with output. If fixed costs remain the same for a given level of output, then within a range of outputs the only additional cost incurred by producing one more unit of service will be the variable cost. The variable cost then represents the marginal cost of the next unit. After a certain level of output, there may be a need to increase fixed costs, in which case the marginal cost at that point will be represented by the variable cost and the increase in fixed costs. This concept is best demonstrated by way of an example.

A prison provides confinement for a maximum of 300 people at full occupancy, although normal occupation rates are 280. The fixed cost of running the prison per annum includes salaries for 80 staff of £1,800,000, accommodation costs of 1,200,000, other fixed costs £400,000. Variable costs have been calculated using the average occupancy rates, including prisoner transport costs of £60,000, meals of £600,000, and other variable costs of £40,000.

Fixed costs are constant for occupancy rates between 200 and 300. Lower occupancy rates would result in lower fixed costs due to consequent staff reductions, whilst higher occupancy rates would result in higher fixed costs as additional accommodation and staff would be required.

Given that the usual occupancy rate is 280, the marginal cost of the 281st person is calculated by identifying what additional costs the prison would have to incur. In this case, since fixed costs are constant whether or not the prisoner is in occupancy, the only additional costs will be the variable costs and therefore the marginal cost is equal to the variable cost. This is calculated as follows:

Total variable costs	£700,000	(Transport, meals and other)
Total number of occupants	280	(Costs based on average occupancy)
Variable cost per person	£2,500	
Marginal cost	£2,500	

The marginal cost of the 301st person would not just be the increase in variable cost, it should also take into account the increase in the fixed costs at that point, as this number exceeds the maximum capacity of the prison.

The marginal cost is useful when there is an opportunity to deliver additional services from the same fixed cost base. For example, the marginal cost of opening a building for more hours than usual will be the variable cost of running the building, i.e. light, heat, contract labour hours, etc. The fixed cost of rent, rates, maintenance contracts, etc. remain the same, open or not. In this example, knowing the marginal cost allows a manager to calculate the cost/benefit of opening for extra hours.

Choosing a Costing Technique

All the above costing techniques can be used in isolation or may be combined. The choice of costing methodology will depend on:

❖ *the extent and quality of data collection undertaken with respect to service delivery. This includes the use of time sheets, activity logs, user records, and so on*

❖ *the complexity of the service*

❖ *the number and range of different activities*

❖ *the type of service user (e.g. purchasers, users who have a legal right to a service, etc.)*

❖ *whether or not the service is being delivered by more than one supplier*

❖ *whether or not the service has to be priced and sold into an internal or external market*

Summary

❑   The unit of service used to calculate a unit cost will be influenced by the type of service, the reason for the costing, and the ease of calculation

❑   There are several methods of unit costing, the most simple being the flat rate approach

❑   Unit costs expressed in terms of hourly rates, tend to be the most commonly used unit of output for professional services, and are relevant for many public sector activities

❑   Standard costing is most often used if there is a specific and routine activity which is repeated in the same way each time

❑   Job costing is most relevant for project work when each assignment is unique

❑   As productivity increases, the unit cost generally decreases as the fixed costs are spread over a larger volume of output. However, beyond a given level of productivity changes in fixed costs will also impact on unit costs

Exercise 5

Calculating Hourly Rates

You have been given the following information about a small team of professionals working within a large public sector organisation.

- Salary rates for individual posts are given below (inclusive of on-costs):

Manager	£30,000
Professional (x 4)	£25,000 (each)
Administrator (x 2)	£15,000 (each)

- Office space is £25 per square foot inclusive, and the team currently use 1200 square foot

- The photocopier lease is £1,200 per annum

- The computers cost a total of £10,000 including software and are expected to become obsolete after 4 years. The maintenance contract has been agreed at £1,000 per year subject to annual re-negotiations

- An estimate of £2,000 has been given for the production of a simple website. This will set out all the information about the service, the team, location, etc.

- Other marketing activities should not exceed £3,000

- A training budget has been calculated based on each member of staff's individual training plan and in total will be £5,000

- Central recharges, for support services such as personnel, have been frozen and will therefore be the same as last year which was £25,000

- The average chargeable hours a year for each professional has been estimated at 1400 hours or 200 days per year. This has taken account of holidays, sickness, and training. Administration is expected to take up 20% of a professional's time and should be reflected in the hourly rates calculated, i.e. they only undertake productive work for 80% of the time

- The manager only has 100 days chargeable per year, with the rest of the time being spent on managing and administering the unit, including attendance at committee meetings, etc.

QUESTION

a) **Based on the assumption that the demand for the service will be consistent during the year and sufficient to occupy all the available productive time, calculate the cost per hour of the professionals and the manager using a flat rate approach. (Assume a 7 hour working day.)**

b) **What changes can be made in order to lower the hourly rate calculated?**

Suggested solutions can be found on page 126

Exercise 6

Cost Per Service Unit

Your team has been asked to calculate how much an initial interview costs per person. Because each interview varies depending on the complexity of the case, interviews have been broken down into three categories as follows:

CATEGORY 1 INTERVIEW

Requires an officer grade or sometimes an assistant and should take two hours on average, with an additional one hour spent reporting

CATEGORY 2 INTERVIEW

Requires an officer grade and may involve more than one. These interviews should on average take four hours with report writing requiring an additional one hour

CATEGORY 3 INTERVIEW

Requires a manager grade with considerable preparation beforehand, with a detailed report. On average, this process may take 14 hours including report writing.

Obviously, time for each category of interview cannot be specified exactly as there are wide variations, so average times have been taken for this costing exercise.

It is assumed that the team will have the following number of interviews during the year:

CATEGORY 1	1,000
CATEGORY 2	630
CATEGORY 3	100

The costs of the team are given as follows:

Staff		
Senior Manager (does not undertake Interviews)		£30,000
Manager Grades (x 2) (50% of time spent on category 3 Interviews)		£50,000
Officer Grades (x 4) (50% of time spent on category 2 Interviews 10% of time spent on category 1 Interviews)		£90,000
Assistants (x 4) (50% of time spent on category 1 Interviews)		£80,000
		£250,000

Car allowances	£15,000	
Travel and subsistence	£5,000	
Premises cost	£20,000	
Other operating expenses	£40,000	
Total overheads		£80,000

TOTAL COST   **£330,000**

In order to calculate costs, it should be assumed fixed overhead costs can be allocated on a pro rata basis according to staff costs and grade.

Using the pro-forma below, calculate the average cost for each type of interview

	Salaries	Proportion of total salaries	Overhead apportionment pro rata	Costs including overhead allocation
Senior Manager	_____	_____	_____	_____
Manager	_____	_____	_____	_____
Officer	_____	_____	_____	_____
Assistant	_____	_____	_____	_____
	_____	_____	_____	_____

Category 1 Interview	£ .... per Interview

Category 2 Interview	£ .... per Interview

Category 3 Interview	£ .... per Interview

Suggested solutions can be found on page 128

Exercise 7

Marginal Costing

A leisure centre provides a number of activities which are subsidised by the local authority. It intends to add a new gym to its range of activities. Assuming 1000 members register each year, the gym will incur the following annual costs.

	Fixed Cost £	Variable Cost £	Total £
Equipment Lease	20,000		20,000
Equipment Maintenance	2,500	500	3,000
Cost of Accommodation (including heat, light, etc.)	5,000		5,000
Sessional Instructors	40,000	2,000	42,000
Gym Manager and Assistant Manager	30,000		30,000
Towels	500		500
Laundry		100	100
Administration	6,500		6,500
Membership Expenses (including cards, etc.)		5,400	5,400
Sundries	1,500		1,500
Total	**106,000**	**8,000**	**114,000**

UNDERTAKE THE FOLLOWING CALCULATIONS:

a)   What is the average unit cost per member, given the target of 1000 members is achieved?

b)   What would be the additional cost of the 1001st member, i.e. the marginal cost?

c)   What is the unit cost if a membership of 1200 is achieved assuming that no additional fixed costs are incurred?

Suggested Solutions can be found on page 130

Exercise 8

Costing Your Own Service

Having established the total cost of your service in exercise 1, consider what would be the most appropriate expression of unit of service and how you would calculate the quantity of units. (E.g. if the choice is hours, whose hours would cost be tied to, and what percentage of hours relate to actual service delivery).

a) Unit of Service

b) Number of Units (Volume/Output)

Attempt to calculate the unit cost for your service based on a) and b)

c) Unit Cost Calculation

d)   Do you consider this cost to be inaccurate or unrealistic? If yes, what reasons would you attribute to your position; tick below:

	✓
Lack of real/accurate data	☐
Not clear of the full range of costs for inclusion	☐
Not sure which costs are central	☐
Not sure how costs have been apportioned	☐
Not sure of the number of units of service	☐
Consider that some costs are not included	☐
Consider that overheads are incorrect - too high/low	☐
Unclear about staff productivity levels	☐
Other: please state	☐

_____

_____

e) What action do you intend to take in order to produce an accurate unit cost?

Action	**Timescale**
_____	_____
_____	_____
_____	_____
_____	_____
_____	_____
_____	_____
_____	_____
_____	_____

Chapter 5

COST CONTROL

Many public sector managers now have to manage and monitor budgets. For some managers this is a new area requiring the development of expertise, however, some managers will have had extensive experience of budgeting over the years. Effective cost control uses the same techniques as budgetary control, but concentrates on the output side of the service, the productivity, as opposed to the financial input to the service, the budget. The process of cost control is reflected in the following diagram:

Process for Cost Control

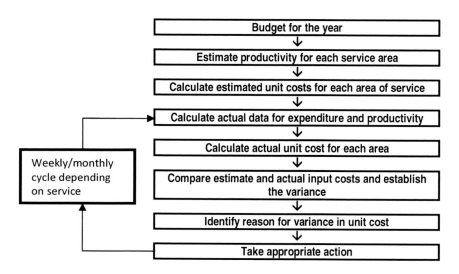

This process is appropriate for any type of unit costing approach, including job costing. Each job should be reviewed in this way on a regular basis, even if it takes several months, or in some cases even years to complete. The work in progress on any particular job has a cost, and this cost should be in line with the estimates of the project plan. If this is not the case, action needs to be taken to ensure the job remains in control and that the cost does not exceed the budget allocation.

Cost control is as essential as budgetary control. A manager may control the budget by not spending beyond the monetary allocations given to the service area, however, if the required level of output is not achieved, this will result in increased unit costs. In this case, budgetary control will have been achieved but costs will be out of control. This is best illustrated with an example as follows:

An environmental health team responsible for the inspection of premises where food is prepared and sold, such as restaurants, has a budget of £300,000. The catchment area has 800 sites that require annual inspection. The salary budget of £150,000 is made up of the salaries for 4 inspection staff, 1 manager and 1 administrator. Travelling costs include leased cars for all staff, except the administrator, and car running costs, total £25,000, other supplies and services including stationery etc. amount to £25,000, and fixed overheads including accommodation equates to £100,000.

Each inspector is responsible for 200 site visits which should on average take 4 hours of the day including journey time, and the remaining 3 hours should be spent producing a report. This allows the inspector enough time to visit each site once per year, with the remainder of the days in the year used on holidays, sickness, meetings and so on. The manager does not undertake site visits but acts as a quality controller, and supervisor.

The estimated standard unit costs have been calculated in two ways:

a) cost per visit 300,000 ÷ 800   = £375
b) cost per hour 300,000 ÷5600 (7x200x4)   = £53.57

The cost per visit has been calculated at a flat rate where the total cost is divided by the number of visits made.

The cost per hour takes into account only the productive time of the inspectors, and assumes the managers cost to be a fixed overhead. The number of hours has been calculated at 7 hours per day for 200 days multiplied by the number of inspectors.

At the year end, the budget has been controlled with actual expenditure amounting to £295,000. However, during the year, due to higher than average levels of sickness and poorly written reports, the numbers of visits made were only 700 for the year, and productive time was 10% below the estimate. Therefore, the actual cost per visit and cost per hour are calculated as:

a) cost per visit 295,000 ÷ 700   = £421.43
b) cost per hour 295,000 ÷ 5040 (5,600x90%) = £58.53

The unit costs are far higher than the estimate due to the reduced productivity.

Cost control becomes particularly important if services are being charged out to third parties. If the environmental health team were under contract to provide inspections, they may have priced their inspections at £400 per visit given that the cost was £375. This would provide a margin for error. However, given that the actual cost per visit was £421.43, the team would have ended up with a deficit on each visit of £21.43.

Variance Analysis

In order to assist with cost control, regular variance analysis should be undertaken. Actual unit costs should be calculated on a monthly basis and compared with the estimated unit cost. To achieve this comparison, information needs to be maintained about the unit of service adopted. In the case of the previous example, statistics would be maintained on the number of visits made and the number of hours worked by each inspector. In this instance, time recording may be useful in providing the detailed information necessary for variance analysis.

Actual monthly costs should be taken from the organisation's financial management system, and each month financial reports should be produced which provide an accurate picture of budgeted versus actual expenditure. These reports are crucial for budgetary control. Actual expenditure reported on the financial systems may require some adjustment to take account of:

Creditors
(Services used but bills unpaid)

Accruals
(Services used but bills yet to be received, e.g. quarterly telephone bills)

Timing differences
(Some costs are not incurred evenly over the year)

The difference between the actual unit cost and the estimated unit cost is called a **variance**. Using information from the previous example, this concept is illustrated as follows:

Environmental Health Team Cost Control
Month 6

a	b	c	d	e	f	g	h	i
Estimated Expenditure for the Month (£)	Actual Expenditure for Month (£)	Variance (1) (£)	Est. Volume Output (Visits)	Actual Volume Output (Visits)	Variance (2)	Est. Unit Cost (£/visit)	Actual Unit Cost (£/visit)	Variance (3) (£)
25,000	24,583	417	66.6	58.3	-8.3	375	*421.66	-46.66

* Slight rounding difference from the previous page

From the above, the variance in each case represents the difference between the estimated and actual figures.

In this table, *column a* takes the overall estimated expenditure for the month. This would be based on the budgeted figures for the service, and should reflect the monthly spending profile for month 6. For ease of calculation, this example assumes a monthly budget of one twelfth of the year's total of £300,000.

Column b shows the actual expenditure for the month. This figure should be based on the monthly financial accounting information including any relevant adjustments, (i.e.

£295,000/12). The difference between these two figures is the expenditure variance shown in *column c*; it is this figure which is most closely reviewed for budgetary control purposes. In this instance the variance is positive, representing an underspend.

Column d shows the estimated service output represented by the estimated number of visits to be undertaken during the month. Again, for ease of calculation a flat rate approach has been adopted which spreads the output evenly during the year (i.e. 800/12). However, as in the case of expenditure, activity should also be correctly profiled to take account of seasonality and demand factors. For example, if the summer months are when most staff take holidays, the estimated output for the summer months would be lower than that of the winter months.

Column e gives the actual output (i.e. 700/12). This information would be obtained from the monitoring sheets kept by staff logging each visit made. The output variance in *column f* is negative showing that there has been a lower than estimated number of visits undertaken during the month.

Column g shows the estimated rate per visit calculated using the flat rate method. The actual rate per visit is calculated in the same manner as the estimate, by taking the actual expenditure and dividing by the actual output. In this scenario, the rate per visit in *column h* is considerably higher than the estimate, and hence there is a large negative variance in *column i*. This result should not be surprising given the negative output variance in *column f* is proportionately greater than the savings on expenditure in *column c*.

It would be expected that if productivity is reduced, then expenditure should also be reduced by the same proportion. If this is the case, the actual unit cost should remain the same as the original estimate.

*For example, continuing the theme of environmental health visits, and given the reduction in actual output from 66.6 to 58.3, monthly expenditure would have to reduce by £3,138 in order to keep the actual cost in **column h** equal to the estimated unit cost in **column g** (i.e. the estimated unit cost is £375 per visit, so the actual cost with the reduced output should only be 58.3 x £375 = £21,862*). This is shown in the following table:*

Month 6

a	b	c	d	e	f	g	h	i
Estimated Expenditure for the Month (£)	Actual Expenditure for Month (£)	Variance (1) (£)	Est. Volume Output (Visits)	Actual Volume Output (Visits)	Variance (2)	Est. Unit Cost (£/visit)	Actual Unit Cost (£/visit)	Variance (3) (£)
25,000	21,862*	3,138	66.6	58.3	-8.3	375	375*	0

* rounded to nearest £

Where the majority of costs are fixed in nature, reductions in output tend to have little impact on the overall service costs. This results in the overall cost reduction required to maintain the estimated unit cost with reduced output, as shown above, may not always be achievable. Hence, reductions in productivity normally have a negative impact on the unit cost variance as shown by the previous example.

Variance reports of this nature could be produced for every type of activity, where a unit cost calculation has been made.

The budget holder must expect to experience variances as it is unlikely that any estimated figure will prove to be 100% accurate. However, there should be a threshold of tolerance outside of which variances require investigation. This may apply to both positive and negative variances. This threshold may be presented in the form of percentages and/or absolute values, and may differ between types of expenditure and types of output.

In addition to monthly activity information, the budget holder should also require year to date or cumulative figures. The cumulative information evens out any major monthly fluctuation and may give a very different impression as compared to the information about any particular month. The cumulative results, i.e. months 1 to 6 in this example, are shown as follows:

Month 6 - Cumulative Results

a	b	c	d	e	f	g	h	i
Estimated Expenditure to date (£)	Actual Expenditure to date (£)	Variance (1) £	Est. Volume Output (Visits)	Actual Volume Output (Visits)	Variance (2)	Est. Unit Cost (£/visit)	Actual Unit Cost (£/visit)	Variance (3) £
150,000*	136,800	13,200	400*	360	-40	375	380	-5

*Figures represent 50% of the annual estimates

The variances are calculated as follows:

Variance (1)	*13,200/150,000*	*x 100*	*=*	*9% (rounded)*
Variance (2)	*-40/400*	*x 100*	*=*	*-10%*
Variance (3)	*-5/375*	*x 100*	*=*	*-1% (rounded)*

The interpretation of the above figures can be summarised as follows:

- It would appear that there is only a small overspend variance on the unit cost of £5, **column i**, which represents a percentage variance of slightly over 1% (see variance (3) calculation), which would probably be within an acceptable tolerance level.
- This is in contrast to the large month 6 overspend variance, shown on the first table of the example, of £46.66.
- The variance on expenditure, **column c**, represents a 9% under spend for the period (see variance (1) calculation), and the variance on output, **column f**, represents a 10% shortfall (see variance (2) calculation).

Therefore, in this example it appears that reductions in productivity are nearly matched by the same proportion of reduction in expenditure. Given the relatively high variances on both expenditure and output, there may still be a need to investigate the reasons for these variances even though the overall unit cost variance is very small.

Corrective Action

In order to take full control of unit costs, the manager must be in control of both expenditure and output as corrective action may be necessary in one or both areas.

Controlling Expenditure

This usually involves monitoring actual expenditure and attempting to remain within pre-set expenditure budgets. Adjustments may need to be made between expenditure headings which balance out to ensure overall expenditure remains within the total budget.

The responsibility for budgetary control may rest at a number of levels:

Senior Management
In the public sector, this level includes the Chief Executive and other Chief Officers and Directors. They will be responsible for ensuring that the whole organisation stays within budget and may have to make budgetary control decisions that appear detrimental to individual departments or services for the sake of the whole. They are unlikely to be involved in detailed day to day control, and will depend on other staff to undertake detailed monitoring of routine expenditure.

Central Finance Officers
If the organisation has central support services, the central finance division will have a role in budgetary control. It will most likely be specifically responsible for financial accounting including the recording of actual expenditure. This information is then compared to budget totals. The extent to which these officers can

influence budgetary control decisions will vary with each organisation.

Departmental Management

Many public sector organisations have decentralised budgets which means that each department has its own budget. The senior management within the department may take total responsibility for the control of this budget, or may further dis-aggregate budgets down to service levels where some of the budgetary control responsibilities are delegated to other staff.

Departmental Finance Officers

These officers will perform a similar role to those at the centre of the organisation. They will constitute   a supporting service for the department and will undertake routine financial and management accounting activities. Such activities will result in the production of the financial management information necessary for budgetary control. The extent to which finance officers make budgetary control decisions will vary from organisation to organisation.

Service Managers

Where an organisation has devolved budgets, the service managers will have the main responsibility for budgetary control. They will be expected to undertake regular monitoring and make budgetary control decisions to ensure expenditure remains within budget. In some organisations, devolvement has not fully taken place and the service manager only has monitoring responsibilities. In such cases, the service manager is unable to make many of the decisions required to adequately control the budget.

In order to effectively control expenditure, the person responsible for budgetary control, should undertake certain processes and make the necessary budgetary control decisions.

These budgetary control processes and decisions are highlighted in the following paragraphs.

Budgetary Control Processes

Budgetary Control Processes	
Accurate budget setting based on future business and service plans (these budgets should be profiled to reflect the patterns of expenditure over the period of the budget, usually one year)	➲ Annually in detail
Regular reviews of financial management information (this will include reviewing budgetary control reports and management accounts)	➲ Quarterly, monthly, or weekly, depending on the nature of the service
Variance analysis (identification of differences between actual and budgeted figures that need to be investigated for cause)	➲ Same frequency as above
Projected outturns (forecasting the year end position based on current expenditure levels)	➲ Every month, quarter, or half-year depending on the nature of the service
Re-forecasts (restatement of original budgets to reflect any changes that need to be made in the light of current expenditure trends)	➲ Same frequency as above

Budgetary Control Decisions

The following are some of the actions required to control over/under spent budgets.

❖ *Decrease/increase expenditure*

❖ *Increase/decrease income*

❖ *Decrease/increase service levels*

❖ *Change the nature of service delivery*

❖ *Delay/bring forward service developments*

❖ *Change the eligibility criteria for free or subsidised services*

❖ *Virement - moving funds from one budget to another, within or across departments, divisions, service areas, or cost centres*

❖ *Use contingency funds if available*

The seniority level at which the above decisions can be made will vary with each organisation. The service manager with devolved responsibility should have sufficient autonomy and control to implement within limits, most of the above actions.

Controlling Output

As with the control of expenditure, the control of output may occur at different staff seniority levels within the organisation. It is likely that the service manager will have to undertake the day to day control of output, as they will be closest to the point of direct service delivery. In addition, service managers will need to ensure staff maximise their productivity. Maximisation of productivity is achieved by:

❖ *High levels of communication*

❖ *Clear guidelines and procedures for service delivery and quality*

❖ *Clear vision of the objectives to be achieved*

❖ *Clear understanding of the functions to be performed*

❖ *Knowledge of the target output levels*

❖ *Training and support*

❖ *High levels of motivation*

❖ *Co-ordination and planning for effective work flow*

❖ *Availability of best possible technical support*

❖ *Appropriate equipment and materials*

❖ *Efficient and effective support services and administration*

To take adequate control of output, the following processes should be undertaken:

❖ *Identify appropriate units of service*

❖ *Set targets for output*

❖ *Collect data on actual output achieved (e.g. time recording)*

❖ *Compare targets and actual - variance analysis*

❖ *Establish reasons for variances* *

    * *Reasons for variances may include:*

- Increased sickness levels
- Lack of resources
- Lack of technical or administrative support
- Over ambitious targets
- Changes in work loads
- Poor staff performance or work ethic
- Lack of skill or ability
- Lack of motivation or low morale
- Better than expected performance

In the event of output falling below target, the corrective action to be taken will depend on the reasons. Potential actions include:

❖ *Changing work flow practices*

❖ *Closer supervision*

❖ *Review of targets*

❖ *Training*

❖ *Disciplinary action*

❖ *Increase in the necessary support*

❖ *Increase in the necessary resources*

Summary

❑ Cost control and budgetary control are both essential in ensuring the delivery of value for money services

❑ Planned unit costs should be compared with actual unit costs and any resulting variances should be investigated on a regular basis

❑ All inputs to the service need to be monitored to establish cost control. Inputs will include not just the financial input represented by the budget but also staff time, equipment, and materials

❑ Corrective action may be required to maintain control. This may be in respect of all factors affecting the unit cost, including finance and productivity

Exercise 9

Cost Control -v- Budgetary Control

Using the list of organisations shown below, identify whether you consider cost control or budgetary control should be more important to the manager stating your reasons why.

Case	Cost Control	Budgetary Control	Reason
Leisure Centre			
School			
Meals on Wheels Service			

Case	Cost Control	Budgetary Control	Reason
Central Personnel			
Architectural Services			
Payroll Services			
Legal Services			
Housing Management Servcies			

Suggested solutions can be found on page 131

Exercise 10

Your Own Cost Control

a)   List the cost control processes you currently adopt
     (e.g. time recording)

b)   Referring to the contents of this chapter, consider
     further actions that could be taken to enhance cost
     control for your service

Chapter 6

PRICING PUBLIC SECTOR SERVICES

Pricing Considerations

There are a number of factors that require consideration when determining a price. These include the following:

❖ *The cost of producing/delivering the goods or service*

❖ *The profit margin to be achieved*

❖ *The prices charged by competitors*

❖ *The market conditions with respect to supply and demand*

❖ *The customers' expectations with regard to payment*

❖ *The way in which payment is made*

❖ *The corporate/organisational policy with regard to price setting*

These issues are discussed below:

Cost

The cost will vary dependent on the type of service to be delivered and the quality and quantity of that service. Costs need to be calculated in such a way that all costs are fully captured in the costing calculation. Chapter 4 sets out the costing methods that may be adopted. Many pricing techniques use the unit cost as a basis for price setting, and therefore accurate costing is fundamental to the price charged.

Profit Margin

Many pricing policies are based on a strategy that allows for a profit margin. The profit margin is the difference between cost and price. In the private sector, profitability is the key to business success, however, the public sector is made up of largely not-for-profit organisations where service quality is usually the key objective. Even so, these organisations may still wish to price services at a rate that allows for a surplus to be generated. Surpluses are required for a variety of reasons including:

❖ *Increase the level of reserves held by the organisation*

❖ *Provide for future investment*

❖ *Act as a contingency for unforeseen events*

❖ *Allow for some services to be subsidised*

Competition

Regardless of the cost base used in calculating a price, if other competitors exist within the market, their pricing strategy also needs to be taken into account when establishing a price level. There is little point setting prices that are considerably higher than the competition unless there are other factors that justify the price differential. For example, the quality, or the location of the service. Changes in government legislation with regard to the way in which public services are delivered, has meant many public services are now delivered by the private or third sectors. This is a growing trend in many countries as governments strive to achieve best value for money from public funds.

Market Conditions

Price is affected by the market conditions of supply and demand. If there are high levels of demand and few suppliers in the market place, prices are driven up, similarly, if there are low levels of demand and many suppliers, prices are driven down.

Customer Expectations

Consumers of goods and services often have an expectation of price based on their previous purchasing experience. If services are priced too far above expectations, customers will not be prepared to pay, similarly if prices are too far below expectations, they may be viewed with suspicion with regards to quality. Customer expectations are influenced by market conditions and competition.

Many public sector services have no direct competition and therefore market price comparisons cannot be readily made by the customer. This is particularly the case where services are funded mainly from central and local taxation. In some cases services are partly funded by direct fees and charges levied on the customer, e.g. library services, day care, etc. Often these contributions do not represent the full cost of the service. Given the growing involvement of the private and third sectors in the delivery of public services, customers will find even fewer areas where some kind of price comparison cannot be made.

Payment

The timing of payment can affect the price level. For example, discounts are offered for quick payment or for bulk purchases, whilst prices are increased for those requiring longer to pay, or payment by instalments. The principal reason for this impact on price is the cost of money. If cash is received quickly, it may be invested to earn interest, or borrowings can be reduced hence saving interest. However, if cash is received slowly, the converse applies. The public sector is affected by cash flow in the same way as the private sector, and some organisations are now introducing incentives and penalties to reflect the timing of payment. The method of payment also affects the speed at which cash can be received, and customers often have the option of paying by some form of credit/debit card, online payment, and other forms of electronic transfer.

Organisational Strategy

Any organisation having to charge a price for goods or services should develop a strategy with respect to pricing. For example, this may involve cross subsidising services by charging high prices for some services and low prices for others. The strategy with respect to pricing will be affected by the organisation's overall goals and objectives. These objectives will cover issues such as profit levels, investment, quality, customers' ability to pay, and so on. An organisation may receive a subsidy in order to keep prices within a certain level. For example, many publicly funded leisure centres are subsidised to ensure prices are structured to allow accessibility for all.

Pricing Techniques

There are a number of pricing methods which may be adopted to develop a price.

Full Cost Recovery

This is where the price is set at the same level as cost; cost should be calculated on a full absorption basis, i.e. the cost covers all fixed costs attributable to the service, as well as the variable costs. This method does not allow for any margin of error and hence, when using full cost recovery, it is wise to build in a contingency figure as part of the fixed cost calculation. Many public sector services will adopt this approach as there is often no necessity to generate a profit.

> *Example*
> *If the cost per hour is £50.00, then the price charged per hour will be £50.00*

Cost Plus

This is the most popular method of price calculation. The cost of the service unit is established, and a "plus" is added. This "plus" amount can be viewed as a profit margin, surplus, contingency, investment, etc. The level of uplift on costs will depend on the impact of the pricing considerations mentioned earlier. Some markets will only allow for very low profit margins, whilst others can achieve very high margins. Where an organisation is a sole provider of services in a particular area, for example, gas, water and electricity, there is scope to adopt a monopoly pricing strategy which allows for very high prices and high profits. However, in such instances there are often independent bodies which help to regulate price.

> **Example**
> **If the cost per hour is £50.00 the cost plus price with a profit margin of 10% will be £55.00**

Cost Minus

This is where price is set below cost. If prices do not recover the cost of service delivery, a loss or a deficit will normally result. There are a number of reasons why an organisation will price a service or product at a loss.

Loss Leader This is where the organisation is trying to capture customers in a new market, or destroy the competition. Prices are set deliberately below the market rate which may require the price to be below cost. Loss leaders are usually part of a short term strategy, and prices are increased when the objective has been achieved.

Spare Capacity An organisation may find that it can provide additional services over and above those needed to cover all its cost. This is known as spare capacity and may have been achieved through increased efficiency. If all fixed costs have been covered, only the variable costs of delivering the service need to be recovered in the price, hence, prices can be set below the normal full absorption cost for the service. (This concept is covered in more detail later in this chapter in the section on break-even.)

> **Example**
> **If the cost per hour is £50.00 which is made up of £40.00 to cover fixed costs and £10.00 to cover the variable costs, then the price for services that use spare capacity could be set as low as £10.00 per hour (i.e. just enough to cover the variable costs)**

Added Contribution In the event that full cost or cost plus prices cannot be achieved due to market conditions, it is sometimes still necessary to sell services at below cost in order to gain some contribution towards fixed costs rather than getting zero contribution. This may be adopted as a short term measure in the hope that market conditions improve, and higher prices may be charged at a future date.

Cross-Subsidy A policy decision may exist to charge less than cost for some services and subsidise any shortfall by charging proportionately more for other services.

Market Rate

This pricing method only takes account of the market place and not the input cost. Prices are set at whatever the market will bear, which will be determined mainly by the forces of supply and demand. When there is high demand and few suppliers of the product or service, this approach allows the provider to charge very high prices, thus achieving high profits. However, these profits may have to be used to subsidise periods of low demand when suppliers then have to lower prices (sometimes below cost). This is quite a common feature of seasonal industry sectors. This type of pricing strategy is not usually suitable for most public services which on the whole are cost driven rather than market led.

Break-even Analysis

Unit costing and pricing is commonly used in the private sector to assist in calculating the "**break-even point**". Break-even arises where there is neither profit nor loss, and income received is equal to expenditure. Break-even is usually expressed in terms of a level of productivity such that the organisation is aware of the number of units of service that need to be delivered in order to break-even. The concept of break-even is explained in the following example:

An information centre has developed its costs for the year as follows:

	Fixed Costs (£)	Variable Costs (£)	Total Costs (£)
Salaries	120,000	30,000	150,000
Accommodation	40,000	-	40,000
Computer access	10,000	10,000	20,000
Other supplies and services	20,000	10,000	30,000
TOTAL	190,000	50,000	240,000

If the unit of service is to be the number of information requests, and the expected number of requests for a year is 10,000, then the average cost per request is £24 (£240,000÷10,000). Therefore, a price that will achieve break-

even would also be £24, this is the full absorption cost price. However, it is normal to adopt a cost plus method of pricing and, therefore, a price of £30 per request may be set; if productivity is according to plan, this price level will yield a surplus.

When the price has been set it is useful to calculate the level of activity necessary to achieve break-even. This figure will assist in monitoring performance, and will indicate the minimum level of productivity to be achieved for financial viability. An example of break-even using the above information is as follows:

The first stage is to calculate the **contribution** made by each unit of service.

CONTRIBUTION = PRICE - VARIABLE COSTS

For each unit of service sold, there is normally a variable cost of service. These costs vary with the level of service and should only be incurred if services are delivered. In this case, the variable cost per unit is £5 (£50,000÷10,000).

CONTRIBUTION = £30 - £5 = £25

Given the above, there is a £25 contribution to fixed costs for every unit sold. Given that the total fixed costs are £190,000, the information centre requires a sufficient volume of contributions to cover this figure, and reach a break-even position.

BREAK-EVEN VOLUME = FIXED COSTS ÷ CONTRIBUTION PER UNIT

That is: **£190,000 ÷ £25 = 7,600**

Even though the estimate for the year is 10,000, the centre must achieve a minimum of 7,600 to break-even, based on a price of £30.

When the number of requests exceeds 7,600, a contribution begins to be made towards profits, e.g. the 7,601st request will contribute £25 to profits.

At the break-even point, the cost per unit is equal to the price per unit. In this example, if 7,600 requests are made during the year, the cost per request will be:

$$\frac{190{,}000 \text{ (fixed costs)} + 38{,}000 \text{ (variable costs of 7,600 x 5)}}{7{,}600}$$

$$=$$

$$£30$$

This is a higher cost per unit than the estimated £24 per request, because at 7,600 requests, productivity is below the estimated 10,000.

Once the break-even volume has been achieved there is scope to reduce prices. Therefore, if break-even is a 7,600 request rate, and there is a capacity to handle 10,000 requests, the remaining 2,400 requests could be charged at a lower rate; the rate would only have to cover the variable cost of £5.

Break-even can be illustrated graphically as follows:

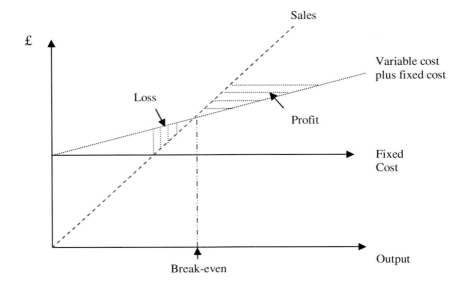

From the above graph, fixed costs are represented by a solid line, variable costs by a dotted line (this starts from the fixed cost line and represents the fact that variable costs are incurred in addition to fixed costs), and sales by a dashed line.

The point where the sales and variable cost lines cross is the break-even point. This represents the volume of sales which provides sufficient revenues to equal the total fixed and variable costs.

When the units of output exceed the break-even number, the graph shows a gap between the sales line and the variable cost line. Where the sales line is higher than the variable cost line, the gap shows the level of profit that is being made for any particular output volume. Similarly, if the volume falls below the break-even point, the variable cost line is above the sales line showing the level of losses incurred.

If a similar graph were plotted for the information service, the fixed cost line for the service would be £190,000, the variable cost line £5 per unit, and the sales line £30 per unit. It would be possible to read from the graph that the break-even volume was 7,600.

These calculations and graph are appropriate if services are being priced and sold into a market place for potential profit. However, many public services do not fall into this category. The income required to deliver the service is by way of an annual budget allocation which is often fixed in nature. In the case of public sector organisations with income represented by a budget allocation, the techniques still apply and the graph can be redrawn as follows:

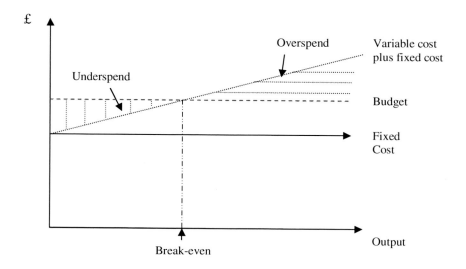

From the graph, the dashed line now represents the budget line instead of sales. As can be seen, this is a straight line representing a fixed budget. Break-even is achieved when this line crosses the variable cost line. If output is above this volume, then the variable cost line exceeds the budget representing an overspend, and if output is below break-even, an underspend is shown. This makes sense, because if a service delivers more service than originally budgeted for, it is likely that more costs will be incurred and hence overspends will ensue.

Graphs can be used as part of the planning and cost control process. It is possible to present different scenarios of cost, price, and break-even by varying the gradients and levels of the various lines until the most realistic position is determined. This can then be used as a monitoring tool where actual performance is plotted against planned performance.

Marginal Costing and Pricing

The marginal cost is the additional cost incurred by increasing output by one unit. This is best explained by an example.

A training department is considering the cost of running a one day training course. They intend to charge a price for the course on a per participant basis and therefore the unit cost has to be developed in the same way. The pricing method is to be cost plus.

The fixed costs per day for the training course include:

	£
Venue hire	150
Equipment hire	50
Trainers fee (1 trainer)	600
Administration	50
General Overhead recovery	50
TOTAL	**900**

The variable cost per person includes:

	£
Training notes	15
Refreshments and lunch	5
TOTAL	**20**

The marginal cost is the difference in total cost when an additional participant is added, e.g. the difference in cost between one participant and two participants. This is set out in the following table which also shows the effect that the increasing number of participants has on the unit cost per participant.

Number of Participants	Fixed Cost	Variable Cost	Total Cost	Marginal Cost	Total Unit Cost (Total Cost/No. of Participants)
1	900	20	920	-	920
2	900	40	940	20	470
3	900	60	960	20	320
4	900	80	980	20	245
5	900	100	1000	20	200
6	900	120	1020	20	170
7	900	140	1040	20	149
8	900	160	1060	20	132
9	900	180	1080	20	120
10	900	200	1100	20	110
11	900	220	1120	20	102
12	900	240	1140	20	95
13	900	260	1160	20	89
14	900	280	1180	20	84

As can be seen from the table, the marginal cost stays constant at £20 per participant and is equal to the variable cost per participant. Therefore, unless fixed costs change, ***the marginal cost will be equal to the variable cost per unit.***

The unit cost per participant decreases with increased volume because the fixed costs are spread over a greater number of units and hence, fixed cost per unit decreases. The converse will be true if volume decreases because fixed cost per unit will then increase.

The training department would expect a course to have an average of 10 participants and have calculated the unit cost from the above table as £110 per person. In order to ensure that there is a margin, the price has been set at £132 per participant. This allows the training department to run the course with only 8 participants and still break-even (where cost equals price). If courses do not attract at least 8 participants it should be cancelled, as losses would then occur.

When the training department has achieved the target of 10 participants per course, they could stimulate further demand by offering additional places at a lower rate. The lowest possible rate would be £20, enough to cover the marginal cost of having an additional participant; any price above the £20 represents a profit element or plus. This approach is referred to as **"marginal cost plus pricing"**.

Internal Charging

A number of public sector organisations have either established or are considering the merits of establishing an internal market place. This means that services delivered by one part of the organisation for another part of the organisation, are charged for as if they had been purchased from a third party supplier. Internal trading allows for more accountability as the provider of services has to ensure that services meet the requirements of the purchasers, otherwise the provider's trading income targets will not be met. Similarly, purchasers know exactly how much internal service is costing and can monitor service quality as well as usage.

In order to establish internal trading within an organisation, the following systems may be required:

Trading Accounts
A trading account is essentially an income and expenditure account and provides a mechanism whereby internal service providers can properly account for income and expenditure

Time (or Other Activity) Recording
Depending on the unit of service to be charged, the service provider has to establish a recording system that can capture the volume of service used by purchasing divisions. Time recording tends to be the most popular type of system as many internal service providers will be charging for service usage in terms of time.

Fee Charging Arrangements
There are a number of charging arrangements that could be implemented. They include:

- internal invoicing,
- monthly journal transfers based on charging records
- monthly journals based on estimates which are adjusted at the end of the year

Flexible Budgets

The service provider will require flexibility in order to react to demand from users. This will include being able to change the budgets using virements (transfers) between budget headings, and to increase and decrease expenditure depending on the income generated.

Carry Forward and Use of Surpluses and Deficits

Internal trading would indicate services are able to create surpluses or incur deficits. There needs to be a system and clear guidelines as to how surpluses and deficits can be carried forward into the following year.

Internal charging is particularly relevant for internal support services such as finance, personnel, legal, and so on. These types of services can be prone to complaints from front line services who sometimes consider support service costs are excessive.

There are clearly advantages and disadvantages in establishing internal trading within a public sector organisation. These are summarised in the following table.

Advantages	Dis-Advantages

Advantages

❖ *Increased accountability*

❖ *Creation of demand led internal services*

❖ *Customers become even more important to service delivery and quality*

❖ *Closer scrutiny of costs by providers and purchasers*

❖ *Increased awareness of trading and the importance of viability*

❖ *Possibility of comparing service with competitors and ensuring value for money*

❖ *Staff incentivised if they trade profitably and profits can be used to benefit the service*

Dis-Advantages

❖ *May need to implement new systems*

❖ *More time spent undertaking additional duties such as keeping time/activity records*

❖ *May be more costly*

❖ *Any profits made are not "real" in terms of the organisation as a whole, as they occur only at the expense of another part of the organisation*

❖ *Increased bureaucracy and paper work*

❖ *Service priorities may move away from providing support to achieving commercial success*

❖ *Some services will never be demanded by purchasers, but need to be provided for the good of the organisation, e.g. "central policy making"*

Cost Reduction Strategies

It is clear that cost is a fundamental ingredient in the determination of price. Pricing public sector services has become critical in the light of an increasing trend towards commercialisation and activities such as competitive tendering and outsourcing.

Competitive tendering and outsourcing of public services, allows organisations from the private and third sectors to bid for contracts to deliver those services. The bidding process will often allow for the existing service providers, which may be an in-house public sector team, to also present a bid. Occasionally existing staff will form their own company and bid as an external bidder, or they may join forces with a third party provider to submit a bid. In all these scenarios, the award of the bid will be determined primarily by price and quality. The weighting of these will vary depending on the type of service. Tendering requires a service specification to be drawn up which forms the basis for bid preparation.

The tendering process often results in savings being achieved, as price submissions for service delivery are often below the current costs being incurred by the in-house team. Even if the in-house team is successful in winning a tender, they may have to dramatically reduce their costs to achieve success.

Cost reduction strategies are essential in order to ensure the long term survival of many services. Cost reduction goes beyond budget cuts, which many in the public sector have to face each year, and addresses productivity, quality and organisational issues.

The types of cost reduction strategies that can be adopted include:

❖ *Examining the way in which services are provided and making changes to working methods and work flow, in order to increase efficiency resulting in the lowering of unit costs*

❖ *Examining the current organisational structure and considering changes which will again increase efficiency but lower fixed costs. For example, the increasing use of flexible working, temporary staff, and short term contract staff. These changes do have difficulties depending on the nature of the service, and have to be carefully considered before implementation*

❖ *Training staff to ensure they are fully conversant with their duties and are achieving a maximum level of output given their capacity. Increasing output in this way will lower unit costs*

❖ *Examining all input costs including equipment and materials and planning their use. Costs can be reduced by:*

  ❖ **Bulk purchasing** - buying larger quantities at reduced prices

  ❖ **Seasonal purchasing** - buying items during low demand periods when suppliers are competing to get sales

❖ **Negotiating discounts** - discounts can be achieved by paying promptly, guaranteeing certain levels of orders throughout the year, using the position of being a large secure public sector organisation

❖ **Purchasing equipment rather than renting it** - this can be useful if the cost of capital is less than the rental costs over the useful life of the equipment concerned

❖ **Purchasing additional guarantees** - often 5 year guarantees can be purchased for a small additional fee, resulting in reduced maintenance and repair costs in future years

❖ **Insuring against risk** - this can be used to reduce the financial impact of unforeseen costs which are difficult to plan for. For example, it is possible to insure against legal claims, breakdown of equipment, etc.

❖ *Close monitoring and control of all areas of expenditure is often the easiest way of identifying areas of cost that have potential for reduction. Cost control methods have been discussed in chapter 5.*

Summary

❑ When establishing a price, one of the key factors that requires consideration is cost. Cost tends to be the basis for most pricing calculations

❑ There are a number of pricing techniques. The most common being "cost plus", where the "plus" represents profit margin, investment or contingency

❑ Break-even is a key concept in costing and pricing; it occurs when a service makes neither profit or loss and when cost is equal to price

❑ Marginal pricing is based on the marginal cost i.e. the cost of one more unit of service. The marginal cost is equal to the variable cost per unit

❑ Internal charging is relevant to those services wishing to establish internal trading relationships with other parts of the organisation

❑ There are a number of cost reduction strategies that may be implemented, in order to lower the cost base and develop more competitive prices

Exercise 11

Pricing Structures

a)   What elements require consideration when developing a price for a police service?

   1) _____

   2) _____

   3) _____

   4) _____

   5) _____

   6) _____

b) Which of the following would be the most appropriate method of charging for a police service? Consider the advantages and dis-advantages of each method before deciding.

Method of Charging	Advantages	Dis-Advantages
Rate per Arrest		
Rates per Hour/Day		
Annual Fee		

Suggested solutions can be found on page 133

Exercise 12

Pricing Calculation

You are required to calculate prices for the services being provided by the mobile library units. There are two mobile library units, and you are given the following information:

a) The total client base will be 20 establishments, each requiring a mobile unit on the premises for one visit per week, assuming a 50 week year.

b) The establishments only appear to be interested in paying for the services on an annual subscription or a rate per visit basis.

c) The mobile library has to replace its total stock every three years. It is assumed that new stock for both units has been purchased by using a one off capital grant of £60,000. Such a grant will not be available in the future.

d) Both mobile units need to be fully maintained and this costs £2,000 per year per unit. Depreciation of the vehicles is £5,000 per year per unit.

e) The average visit to an establishment requires a round trip journey of 10 miles which costs £5 in terms of physical running costs such as petrol.

f) The staff costs including all on costs are made up as follows:

Co-ordinator	£25,000
Administrator	£15,000
2 Library Officers	£40,000
Temporary Staff	£4,000

g)   Other costs have to be incurred as follows, rent £6,000 per annum, heat and light at £1,500 per annum, computer depreciation at £2,000 per annum, telephone at £2,500 per annum, other expenses (including staff training, finance and personnel support services and so on) £5,000 per annum.

h)   Having undertaken a marketing course, the co-ordinator knows the unit will require a marketing budget; this will mainly be used for website maintenance, promotional activities such as email marketing and producing printed information. It is estimated that £5,000 per year will be needed.

i)   Having taken all the costs into account, there is an administration cost for setting up and maintaining an establishment (or any other type of client) on the register. This works out to be £500 per client per year regardless of how often the service is used.

j)   The service has to attempt to make a surplus so that it can invest in its future development. Therefore, a 20% uplift on costs must be made and reflected in the price.

PLEASE CALCULATE THE FOLLOWING:

a)   The annual subscription price that should be charged per establishment for using the mobile library service

b)   The price per visit to be charged for using the mobile library service

Suggested solutions can be found on page 134

Exercise 13

Break-even

Social Services now provide services such as residential care for the elderly at a price. They have recently acquired a new establishment for up to 30 residents. The fixed cost for the establishment is £750,000 and variable costs are £10,000 per person. The price being charged is £40,000 per person per year.

Given this information, plot a graph and determine the number of residents required in order to break-even.

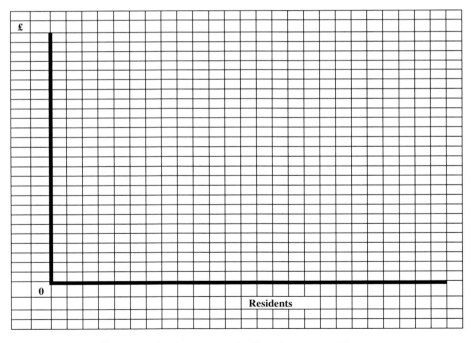

Suggested solutions can be found on page135

Exercise 14

Your Price

a) If you have set, or are about to set a price for your service, how do you intend to calculate the price? (Tick where appropriate.)

Equal to cost   ❑

Cost plus   ❑

if so, what level of uplift will be made   _____

Market rate   ❑

Other - please specify   _____

b) Given the type and quality of service you deliver, do you consider that your price represents good value for money? (Tick where appropriate.)

Yes ❑   No ❑

If the answer is yes, state how you know and how this has been achieved. If the answer is no, identify how, if at all, the price could become good value for money

_____

_____

_____

_____

_____

c) Do you consider that your price is competitive? (Tick where appropriate.)

Yes ❏   No ❏

If the answer is yes, state how you know and how this has been achieved. If the answer is no, identify how, if at all, the price could be made competitive

_____

_____

_____

_____

_____

Chapter 7

COMMON COSTING AND PRICING PROBLEMS ANSWERED

This chapter sets out a number of typical problems that managers may encounter in costing and pricing services, and then gives suggested answers with practical solutions.

Problem 1
We are unable to identify clear units of service as each task we undertake is unique. We concentrate on the care of individuals which cannot be uniformly packaged in the same way as products.

ANSWER 1

The unit of service should be defined on the same basis as the *performance measure* for the service. This may be stated in terms of outputs or inputs. In the above scenario, the unit would relate to the number of individuals cared for, or the time spent on caring for those individuals, i.e. hours. It would be useful to calculate both types of unit cost which will indicate the following.

Cost per client   ⇨   Indicates the level of output from the service

Cost per hour   ⇨   Indicates the level of input to the service and productivity levels of staff

The problem states that each task undertaken is unique, which may also indicate that different tasks have different values and that there are very different levels of input to each individual case. In order to make a costing exercise worthwhile in these circumstances, it is perhaps useful to adopt a job costing approach, where each case is looked upon as an individual job. The output cost of the service is then calculated by adding the cost of all the inputs, including the time spent and hourly rates of the staff concerned with the case.

Problem 2

We wish to reduce costs in order to become more competitive, but all our costs are very high and fixed in nature. Our hands are tied with respect to our two main areas of cost; accommodation and staffing. If we were allowed total autonomy we are sure that we could cut our costs by up to 30%.

ANSWER 2

The first task to be undertaken is to identify exactly why the service is uncompetitive and which elements of the fixed costs are substantially more than the competitors. When public sector organisations begin to compare pay rates with private sector rivals they may find pay levels are similar for certain jobs. The key difference is often the level of productivity and the benefits enjoyed by public sector workers which may include longer holidays, longer periods of paid sick leave, other types of compassionate leave, overtime payment or time off in lieu.

The key to making salary costs more competitive is through increased productivity. Increased productivity from all staff will allow the service to make efficiency savings through reduced unit costs, and may enhance the quality of service being delivered. A higher service cost can only be justified if there are substantial differences in quality when comparing the service to that of a competitor.

Public sector organisations often have little choice with respect to accommodation, as corporately owned property has to be occupied even if accommodation is cheaper elsewhere. There is no saving achieved by services moving out, as the organisation still has to pay for the existing building in addition to any new accommodation. Costs can be reduced by considering how the space is utilised. Some large private sector companies employ specialists to plan the use of floor space in order to maximise their utilisation as part of cost control, and the same approach can be adopted in the public sector.

Many in the public sector consider that they could operate more effectively and competitively outside of the confines, policies and procedures of their organisation. However, there are benefits to be gained from being part of a large organisation, such as economies of scale, organisational support systems, corporate image, and so on; any attempt to move outside the organisation will have to take the loss of these benefits into account.

There are other cost reduction strategies that have been discussed in chapter 6 of this book which can also be adopted in order make a service more competitive.

Problem 3
The costing process for our division will need to be very complex because of the wide range of different services we deliver. We have no expertise in costing, and we do not have the time or resources needed to undertake the necessary calculations and the requirements of the subsequent monitoring and control.

ANSWER 3

A division that offers a wide range of services requiring different costing methodologies may have a difficult task, particularly if there are no skilled personnel to undertake the initial setting up stage. One simplistic approach would be to find a common denominator for all the services provided. This will most probably be *time*. This can be a starting point for more complicated costing at a later stage.

Establishing a cost per hour for each grade of staff can be performed in a simplistic flat rate manner to begin with. This can then be enhanced to take account of other factors affecting each job such as expected productivity levels. Having established hourly rates, a time recording system has to be put in place. Such a system does not have to be time consuming and expensive and may be as simple as keeping a diary.

The time recording system should produce data for collation and analysis and provide the manager with the following types of information:

❖ *Actual cost per hour*

❖ *Actual cost per activity, based on the number of hours spent on each area*

❖ *Productivity levels per staff member based on number of hours of productive time*

Reviewing this information is useful in the monitoring and control of the service, and can assist the manager to save time and resources by having a clear understanding of the performance being achieved in each area of activity.

It is not necessary to be an expert in costing to begin a costing process. If the division is part of a large organisation, there should be assistance available from some of the support service providers. Although initially it may appear to be a high investment in time and resources, having a costing process in place tends to be very worthwhile in the long run.

Problem 4

No one wants to complete time sheets. Is there another way of obtaining information about a service that depends mainly on professionals giving their time?

ANSWER 4

Time sheets are a curse for many people, especially if they appear complicated to complete. It is often said, "where do I put down the time it has taken to complete the time sheet?!"

Unfortunately there is no simple way to capture the cost of using professional time other than by using some form of time analysis, and the only way to analyse time, is by recording how it is used.

Time recording systems tend to involve the completion of time sheets (paper based or on-line) which are usually part of a computerised processing system which can analyse the data automatically. These systems have in-built analysis functions which produce various management reports for monitoring purposes. There other time recording approaches such as swipe cards, barcodes, signing in /out mechanisms, etc.

The time sheet can be made easier to complete and less time consuming if there is:

❖ *a clear split between productive and non-productive time*

❖ *a coding system for identifying different activities*

❖ *no need to calculate totals*

❖ *a requirement to complete them at least weekly, if not daily*

❖ *a minimum requirement to write descriptions*

❖ *sufficient scope to analyse all types of time, particularly with respect to non-productive areas*

Problem 5

As a support service, what is the point of pricing our service and charging other departments within the organisation? It appears to be a paper chasing exercise as our service is not sold outside in the market place and other departments will have to cover our costs regardless. The exercise of costing and pricing appears to be a waste of time and effort!

ANSWER 5

In many public sector organisations, support services are criticised by other parts of the organisation for being an expensive overhead. The process of costing and pricing these services can help to change this image. Even if there is a policy within the organisation of always recovering the full cost of support services, it is important to have a clear indication of what the services are costing and whether or not value for money is being achieved. By making users more aware of their costs, costing and pricing of services will assist users to act more like customers; they will pay more attention to quality, quantity, deadlines, etc., when they are aware of what the service is costing.

The support service will itself benefit by establishing its cost and level of charges and being confident that the service is not expensive when compared to similar service providers in the private sector. This often proves to be the case as there is no profit margin to be recovered for an internal service, and the service can set charges equal to cost.

A costing and pricing exercise does not have to result in a great amount of paper generation. It is quite common to formulate service level agreements between service providers and users, to identify exactly what level of service is to be performed and the cost of that service. When such an agreement has been reached, very uncomplicated charging processes can be introduced such as a monthly flat rate. This charge can be initiated without documentation but by way of journal transfer from the user's budget to the providers budget. Other, more complex charging methods have been described in chapter 6.

It is unlikely that costing and pricing will be a waste of time and effort, but more of an enlightenment highlighting areas that may need to change in order to create better value for money or to prepare for potential competition, even if the service is not currently operating in a competitive environment.

Problem 6
We know we cost more than the private sector equivalent, but we are sure we provide better value for money due to the high quality of service delivery. How can we prove it?

ANSWER 6

Quality should have a value, but in any service it is often difficult to identify the cost of quality. One approach to identifying the cost of quality is to draw up a detailed specification for the service that is currently provided. That specification should then be compared with the specification for the service provided by the private sector equivalent. The differences in the specification should be identified and costed, and can then be cited as the cost of quality.

In addition, the cost of quality as calculated above can be deducted from your service cost to achieve a comparable cost to the private sector equivalent. This would identify whether or not your service is competitive on a like for like basis.

Problem 7
We want to undertake a costing exercise, but it is impossible to capture all the relevant costs. No one seems clear about what overheads we use and how much support services really cost.

ANSWER 7

The key to establishing appropriate unit costs is to identify all the costs relevant to the service. It is also useful to split these costs between fixed and variable costs. Overheads are usually fixed in nature.

A starting point to the costing exercise with respect to establishing overheads is to identify the types of overhead that would be incurred in order to deliver the service. Other support and central service costs, should also be added. This should provide a comprehensive list of cost areas.

To establish the cost of each area, the following steps can be taken

❖ *Identify the volume of overhead utilised*

❖ *Establish the unit costs of those overheads, e.g. accommodation cost per square foot, support service cost per hour, etc. If this is not currently available from the providers, an estimate should be obtained*

❖ *Service level agreements should be entered into wherever possible for support services*

❖ *Lobby decision makers to introduce costing generally for all service providers*

If none of the above steps can be taken, estimates should be made based on any available historic data with respect to overhead costs and charges made by support services and central services. These costs would have been charged to the service at some stage, most probably at the year end when the accounts are being prepared. These charges may not be based on usage but on an arbitrary method of apportionment.

Another approach is to gain estimates for overhead costs and support services from third party suppliers. These independent figures could also be used to gain an approximation of the overhead cost of the service.

SOLUTIONS TO EXERCISES

Solutions to Exercises

Solution to Exercise 1
Types of Cost

Note: Some items have ticks in both the direct and indirect boxes because depending on the circumstances, they could be classified in either category

Area of Expenditure	Fixed Cost	Variable Cost	Direct Cost	Indirect Cost	Controllable Cost	Uncontrollable Cost (in the short term)
Salaries (full time staff)	✓		✓	✓		✓
Employee on costs	✓		✓	✓		✓
Wages (full time staff)	✓		✓	✓		✓
Overtime		✓	✓	✓	✓	
Agency fees (temp. staff)		✓	✓	✓	✓	
Travel to clients		✓	✓		✓	
Leased cars	✓			✓		✓
Rent	✓			✓		✓
Repairs	✓		✓	✓	✓	✓ Depending on severity
Cleaning office premises	✓			✓		✓ If under contract
Security	✓			✓		✓ If under contract
Marketing	✓		✓	✓	✓	
Printing	✓		✓	✓	✓	
Stationery	✓		✓	✓	✓	
Postage to clients		✓	✓		✓	
Equipment rental	✓		✓	✓		✓ If under contract
Telephone calls	✓	✓	✓	✓	✓	
Sundries	✓			✓	✓	
Support service recharge	✓			✓		
Debt charges	✓			✓		

Solution to Exercise 3
Allocating Costs

Service Department	Employee Numbers	Personnel Cost £'000	Employment Costs £'000	Personnel Cost £'000	Budget Size £'000	Personnel Cost £'000
1	200	80	4,000	108	8,000	143
2	250	100	3,500	95	8,000	143
3	390	156	3,900	105	6,500	116
4	160	64	3,600	98	4,000	71
5	125	50	1,500	41	3,000	54
6	400	160	6,000	163	7,000	125
7	325	130	5,200	141	5,800	104
8	150	60	1,800	49	2,500	44
Total	2,000	800	29,500	800	44,800	800

- There are rational arguments for using any of the above methods of apportionment

- They are all arbitrary and do not reflect the usage of the service

- The most common choice for personnel services is employee numbers

Solution to Exercise 5
Calculating Hourly Rates

a) **The total cost of the service is calculated as follows:**

	£
Manager	30,000
Professionals	100,000
Administrators	30,000
Office space (1,200 sq ft @ £25 per sq ft)	30,000
Lease	1,200
Computer depreciation (£10,000 ÷ 4 years)	2,500
Computer maintenance	1,000
Website and Marketing	5,000
Training	5,000
Recharges	25,000
Total	**229,700**

Total hours available:

Professionals:	4 x 1,400 x 80%	=	4,480
Managers:	7 hrs x 100 days	=	700
			5,180

Hence, the flat rate calculation of the hourly rate is:

229,700 ÷ 5,180 = **£44.34 per hour**

b) **The changes which can be made in order to lower the hourly rate calculated include:**

- *Reducing the level of non-productive professional staff hours*

- *Increasing the productive hours of the manager*

- *Reduce the level of controllable costs such as marketing and training*

Solution to Exercise 6
Cost Per Service Unit

	Salaries	Proportion of total Salaries	Overhead Apportionment pro rata	Costs Including overhead allocation
Senior Manager	30,000	12%	9,600	39,600
Manager	50,000	20%	16,000	66,000
Officer	90,000	36%	28,800	118,800
Assistant	80,000	32%	25,600	105,600
	£ 250,000	100%	£ 80,000	£ 330,000

Category 1 Interview	$\dfrac{(105,600 \times 50\%) + (118,800 \times 10\%)}{1,000}$	**£64.68 per interview**

Category 2 Interview	$\dfrac{118,800 \times 50\%}{630}$	**£94.29 per interview**

Category 3 Interview	$\dfrac{66,000 \times 50\%}{100}$	**£330.00 per interview**

An alternative approach would be to add the senior manager's salary to the overhead costs, and absorb the total overheads within the cost of the remaining three grades. This would yield the following costs per interview.

	Salaries	Proportion of Total Salaries	Overhead Apportionment pro-rata	Costs including Overhead Allocation
Manager	50,000	22.7%	24,970	74,970
Officer	90,000	40.9%	44,990	134,990
Assistant	80,000	36.4%	40,040	120,040
	220,000	100%	*110,000	330,000

*This includes the senior manager's salary of £30,000 now treated as an overhead

Interview 1	$\dfrac{(120{,}040 \times 50\% + (134{,}990 \times 10\%)}{1{,}000}$	**£73.52 per interview**

Interview 2	$\dfrac{134{,}990 \times 50\%}{630}$	**£107.13 per interview**

Interview 3	$\dfrac{74{,}970 \times 50\%}{100}$	**£374.85 per interview**

Solution to Exercise 7
Marginal Costing

a) Unit cost per member $= \dfrac{114,000}{1,000} = £114.00$

b) Marginal cost of additional members $= \dfrac{8,000}{1,000} = £8.00$

c) Unit cost for 1,200 members $= \dfrac{114,00 + (200 \times 8)}{1,200} = £96.33$

Solution to Exercise 9
Cost Control -v- Budgetary Control

It should be noted that controlling costs and controlling budgets are both extremely important and that in some cases it may be difficult to decide which takes priority.

Case	Cost Control	Budgetary Control	Reason
Leisure Centre	✓		Depends on income generation from activities which cover costs, e.g. the number of exercise classes held depends on the cost per class versus volume of tickets sold.
School	✓		Funding relates to the number of pupils and so the cost per pupil needs to be controlled to ensure it is within funding allowances
Meals on Wheels Service	✓		Cost per meal will be the measure which determines the gross profit margin, and this needs to be controlled especially if the price per meal is fixed
Central Personnel		✓	If there are no trading accounts and the costs are recharged, then the service needs to ensure the net expenditure is controlled

Case	Cost Control	Budgetary Control	Reason
Architectural Services	✓		Architects fees are controlled by rules and guidelines and by market conditions. This means productivity and output, i.e. cost control, will be essential in order to be viable in competition
Payroll Services	✓		The market place tends to look at payroll in terms of cost per employee. This needs to be controlled, however the cost is nearly all fixed, particularly the cost of the computer system and staff. In order to be competitive, the volume needs to be controlled/ expanded to lower unit costs
Legal Services	✓		This used to be a service where only expenditure needed to be controlled, but now hourly rates will be most important and individual productivity will have to be controlled
Housing Management Servcies	✓		Cost per dwelling may be one of the measures used to compare providers in order to identify value for money

Solution to Exercise 11
Pricing Structures

a) 1) *Cost of the service*
    2) *Way in which service is provided*
    3) *Who the service is provided for*
    4) *Alternative sources of service provision*
    5) *Level of demand for the service*
    6) *How the service can be paid for*

b)

Method of Charging	Advantages	Dis-Advantages
Rates per Arrest	■ Prices based on successful outcomes ■ Easily monitored ■ Forces providers to reach targets to earn sufficient income to survive	■ Wide fluctuations in arrest rates, therefore difficult to estimate volumes and therefore difficult to give an average price ■ Service provider will be incentivised to obtain highest numbers by whatever means possible ■ Does not emphasise quality, only quantity of service ■ Does not take account of the range of services delivered
Rates per Hour/Day	■ Averages productivity, as more days delivered the more fees are generated ■ Easily monitored with time sheets ■ Useful price to compare with other similar service providers	■ No incentive to control how much time is spent on particular aspects of the service ■ Problems could occur if number of days required to deliver the service cannot be afforded
Annual Fee	■ Easy to determine as based on annual cost ■ Can offer a complete range of services and concentrate on quality of service ■ Fixed income which ensures costs are controlled within this figure	■ No way to ensure output targets are met ■ Fixed fee for the whole year restricts opportunities for expansion

Solution to Exercise 12
Pricing Calculations

The first step is to identify the fixed and variable costs

FIXED COSTS	**£**
Salaries	84,000
Stock Write Down (60,000 ÷ 3)	20,000
Maintenance	4,000
Depreciation of Vehicles	10,000
Rent	6,000
Heat and light	1,500
Depreciation of Computer	2,000
Telephone	2,500
Marketing	5,000
Other	5,000
TOTAL	**140,000**

VARIABLE COSTS	**£**	
£5 per trip, each establishment		
requiring 50 trips	250	
Admin. costs for the year	500	
	750	per establishment

TOTAL COSTS

Fixed Costs	140,000
Variable Costs 20 x £750	15,000
	155,000
20% Surplus	31,000
TOTAL	**186,000**

i) *Subscription price per* 186,000/20 = **_£9,300 per year_**
   Establishment

ii) *Price per visit* 9,300/50 = **_£186 per visit_**

Solution to Exercise 13
Break-even

The graph is plotted from the following data:

Residents	Fixed cost £'000	Variable Cost £'000	Total Cost £'000	Sales Revenue £'000
5	750	50	800	200
10	750	100	850	400
15	750	150	900	600
20	750	200	950	800
25	750	250	1,000	1,000
30	750	300	1,050	1,200

Total Cost = Sales Revenue @ 25 residents

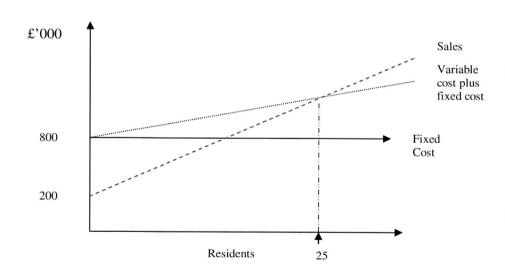

Continued next page

135

Break-even is reached when the establishment has an occupancy of 25 residents.

This could be calculated as follows:

	£
Price	40,000
Variable Cost	10,000
Contribution	**30,000**

$$\frac{\text{Fixed Cost}}{\text{Contribution}} = \text{Break-even} \quad \frac{750,000}{30,000} = 25 \text{ Residents}$$

INDEX

A

B

C

D

E

F

G

H

I

J

L

M

N

O

For further information see www.hbpublications.com
and www.fci-system.com